Core Knowledge®

ISBN: 978-1-68380-346-1

Immigration

Table of Contents

Reader

Core Knowledge History and Geography™

Chapter 1
A Nation of Immigrants

A Mixture of Peoples By the year 2060, the population of the United States is expected to grow to more than four hundred million people. With the exception of Native Americans, the people who live in the United States are generally the **descendants** of immigrants, or immigrants themselves. No wonder one historian wrote, "The history of America is **immigration**."

The Big Question

What were the various causes of mass migration to America?

Another scholar makes the same point in a different way. He offers this prediction: three hundred or four hundred years from now, future historians will find it hard to believe that back in the 1800s and 1900s, people from different continents and dozens of different countries would come together to form a nation that not only would survive, but would become a shining example to the rest of the world.

Vocabulary

descendant, n. someone who is related to a person or group of people who lived in the past

immigration, n. the act of coming to live permanently in a new country

America has a long history of immigration. For several hundred years now, people from all over the world have settled here. Many Americans can trace their ancestors to different parts of the world. Of course, Native Americans lived here long before these immigrants arrived.

The First European Immigrants

North America has been home to Native Americans for thousands of years. In many ways they were the first immigrants. But the story of immigration to America, as we tell it today, begins with Europeans who started colonies in North America. You may not have thought of the settlers of colonial Jamestown, Plymouth, and the Massachusetts Bay Colony as immigrants, but they were. So were the thousands of other colonists who settled throughout the thirteen British colonies. And so were the thousands more who settled in Spain's colonies in the southwestern part of today's United States.

You may remember that, even in those early years, settlers in America came from many different lands. Most were from England, but there were Germans, Dutch, Scots-Irish (Scots who had been living in Northern Ireland), Swedes, Finns, French, Swiss, and others as well. And of course, there were those many, many thousands of Africans who were forced to come to the Americas against their will.

For about a half-century after independence—from the 1770s through the 1820s—immigration to America slowed down. There were two main reasons why. One was because during many of those years, European countries were at war with each other. They fought each other on the seas as well as on land, and they didn't much care about anyone who got in the way. That made traveling on the oceans dangerous. Anyone thinking of leaving Europe to live in America would have to think twice before making that voyage.

The second reason was that those same warring nations made it difficult for their citizens to leave. Their governments believed that losing population would weaken their ability to carry on the wars. Several European governments tried to stop **emigration** altogether.

Eventually, though, both of those barriers fell. By the 1830s, the movement of immigrants to

> ## Vocabulary
>
> **emigration,** n. the act of leaving one country to settle permanently in another

America became a steady stream. In the twenty years after that, it became a mighty river. How mighty? Think of this: by 1860, just before the start of the Civil War, more than one out of every eight persons living in the United States—one out of eight—was born somewhere else.

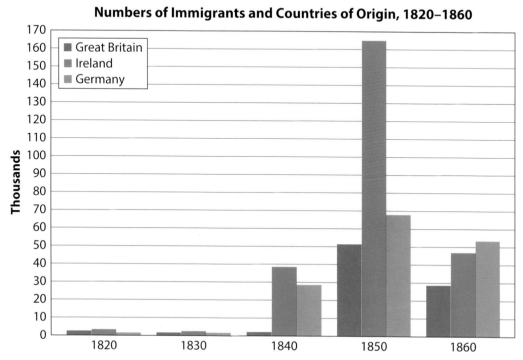

Numbers of Immigrants and Countries of Origin, 1820–1860

As you can see, during this time period most of the immigrants to the United States came from Ireland and Germany. After the Civil War, significant numbers of people from places such as Italy and Scandinavia came too.

Old Immigration, 1820–1860

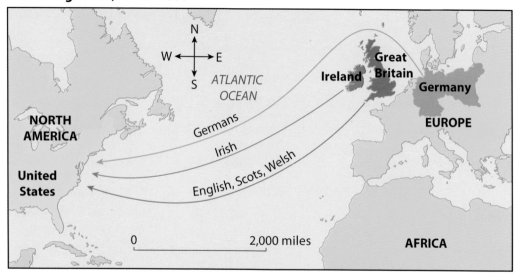

The "Push" to Emigrate

Why were so many people ready to give up everything familiar—their hometowns and villages, often their families, and almost always their friends—for life in a strange new land? Obviously, the reasons were not the same for all who came. In general, though, we can say there was a "push" and a "pull" in each person's decision to set off for America.

The main "push" for most immigrants was **economic**. At that time, the great majority of people in every European country, as well as everywhere else in the world, made a living by farming. Between 1750 and 1850, the population in western Europe doubled, but the amount of farmland did not. That meant that farming families had to make do with less land.

Working on smaller plots—and, remember, without the aid of modern fertilizers and farming equipment—families with farms found it harder and harder to grow enough food for their needs, even under the best of conditions. A bad turn in the weather, a crop disease, or anything that reduced the harvest could spell disaster for them.

That is what happened to countless German farmers. Farming smaller plots of land, many of them had begun to slide into poverty by the 1830s. Some left for the nearby cities, but many headed straight for the United States. Even some of the better-off farmers left, for they could see how **vulnerable** they were. When crop failures struck in the 1840s, hundreds of thousands more German farmers left.

> **Vocabulary**
>
> **economic,** adj. relating to the management of money and resources to produce, buy, and sell goods and services
>
> **vulnerable,** adj. lacking protection; likely to be hurt physically or emotionally; weak

The problem in Ireland was even worse. For years, Irish farmers survived to some extent by growing potatoes on tiny plots of rented land. In the 1800s, two disasters struck. One was the decision of landowners to convert their lands from growing crops to raising sheep. Because fewer workers were needed to raise sheep than to grow crops, about a million Irish were thrown off the land. More than half of them left for America between 1815 and 1845.

Vocabulary

blight, n. a disease that causes plants to dry up and die

The second disaster struck in 1846. A disease known as potato **blight** wiped out nearly the entire crop for several years in a row. Starvation was everywhere. "There will be nothing for us but to lie down and die," said one poor woman. A person making a return visit to one Irish town in 1847 wrote about what he saw:

> Out of a population of 240 I found thirteen already dead from want. The survivors were like walking skeletons—the men gaunt and haggard, stamped with the livid mark of hunger—the children crying with pain—the women in some of the cabins too weak to stand.

Over the next several years, more than a million more Irish left for America.

EJECTMENT OF IRISH TENANTRY.

When they were no longer needed to work the land, poor Irish farmers and their families were thrown out of their simple homes to fend for themselves. When the potato blight wiped out their main food source, with nowhere to live and nothing to eat, one million people died of starvation and disease.

In a few countries, there was another economic "push" factor. In Great Britain and in some of the German lands, industrialization—making goods in factories with the aid of machines—had begun. In time, factories would mean more jobs, not fewer. But in the early stages of the factory system, machines replaced skilled workers, leaving them without jobs. Some took jobs in the new factories, but many others chose to leave their homeland.

Religious and political persecution were, for some, also push factors. Protestant groups, such as the Mennonites and the Amish, were eager to flee religious persecution in Germany. In addition, liberals who had supported the revolutions that swept through Europe in 1830 and 1848 often felt they had to leave after those revolutions failed.

The "Pull" of America

What about those "pull" factors that attracted so many of these people to America? What ideas did these future immigrants have about America, and where did they get them?

Newspapers and books were two important sources of information. Europeans were extremely curious about this newest of nations, and their newspapers regularly carried stories about life in the United States, as well as ads posted by American businessmen who hoped to attract cheap European labor. Several hundred European visitors returned to write books about their travels. They even published guidebooks about the new land in half a dozen languages.

Most important, though, were the letters written by relatives and friends who had already moved to America. These letters have come to be called the American letters. They were passed from one member of a family to another. They were published in local newspapers and read aloud to groups that assembled in the village centers.

Read the words of these earlier immigrants and you will have no trouble understanding why a struggling European farmer or town worker would consider giving up everything and moving:

From an Englishman in New Hampshire—We now have a comfortable dwelling and two acres of ground planted with potatoes, Indian corn, melons, etc. I have two hogs, one ewe [female sheep] and a lamb: cows in the spring were as high as 33 dollars, but no doubt I shall have one in the fall.

From a Dutch woman in Massachusetts—Nearly all people eat three meals a day . . . Arnhem [a Dutch city] can't compare with it. One sees no poor here. . . . Schools are free . . . there are no taxes. . . . The finery is great, one cannot discern [see] any difference between the cobbler's wife and the wife of a prominent gentleman . . . nobody steals here . . . no night watchman.

From a Norwegian in New York—Those who are willing to work will not lack employment or business here. It is possible for all to live in comfort and without want.

From a German in Missouri—Tell Miriam there is no sending children to bed without supper, or husbands to work without dinner in their bags.

From a Swede in Illinois—This is a free country and nobody has a great deal of authority over another . . . nobody needs to hold his hat in his hand for anyone else.

From a Welshman in New York—Dear wife, . . . If you will let the two eldest boys come over to me for a while it will be of great benefit to them. They will be taught for nothing until they are fourteen years old. Here are the best schools in the world at the cost of the state.

From a Norwegian in New York—Our son attends the English school and talks English as well as the native-born.

Letters like these led to the outbreak of what came to be called American fever. Sometimes the fever struck an entire village and carried away many of its residents to America. People from all over the world looked to this new country, and many did whatever they could to get there. And so, by 1860, America had become the new home for so many.

Of course, not all the letters home were so positive about America. Some immigrants reported back that they couldn't get jobs because they didn't know English. Others wrote that things weren't nearly as good in America as they had expected them to be. And there were those who simply could not bring themselves to tell folks back home just how tough things were for them. They said nothing at all.

Such letters may have dampened enthusiasm for America for a while. But then would come another letter with money, perhaps as a gift to help relatives who had stayed behind, perhaps for buying a ticket to America. A single money order from a new American might be more than a European villager would see in years of hard work. American fever would rise all over again.

People came to America for many reasons. Some were escaping religious persecution, hunger, and poverty. Others were lured by American fever. Some immigrants settled easily in their new home, but for many, the first years in America were very challenging.

Cheaper Passage

By the 1850s, large steamships were replacing sailing ships, so the cost of traveling to America began to drop. It cost an English or Irish immigrant of that time only one-fourth as much to get to America as it had cost those from the same lands thirty years earlier.

And so they came—two million from Ireland, another six hundred thousand from England, Wales, and Scotland. German immigrants numbered well over a million, and French another two hundred thousand. Norway, Sweden, the Netherlands, and Switzerland—all provided many thousands of new Americans. During the years before the Civil War, one hundred thousand French Canadians came across the border into our northern states, while forty thousand Chinese arrived on our western shores.

Some of these immigrants were driven by desperation, some by a desire to improve their lives, some no doubt by a spirit of adventure, and surely some by the search for freedom and equality. Whatever their motive, they were brave souls, all of them, striking out boldly to start over in a strange new world.

Chapter 2
Starting Over

Difficult Voyage Before beginning life in America, nearly all immigrants first had to endure the hardships of an ocean voyage. Sailing to America in the early 1800s was not as risky as it had been in colonial times, but it was hardly a pleasure cruise.

The Big Question

How was life different for immigrants who came to America with some money, or had a skill, from those who were poor farm workers?

If people became sick during the voyage, there was little that could be done—unless the immigrant had money. Even then, there wasn't a great deal of medical care available on board the ships.

The voyage lasted anywhere from one to three months, depending on wind and weather. The sailing ships on which they traveled were made for carrying **freight**, not passengers. Ship owners

made good money simply by putting fifty bunk beds into a huge airless room below deck and selling tickets to immigrants—often as many as 250 or more—who would take turns using the bunk beds. On good days, passengers could walk above deck and enjoy the fresh sea air. On bad or simply cold days, though, they stayed below, breathing stale air and often getting seasick.

On many ships, passengers were expected to provide their own food and prepare it on a single large stove shared by all. Those who failed to bring enough food might buy some from the ship's captain, but at sky-high prices. Otherwise, they had to get along on what they brought and on whatever amount of drinking water the captain provided.

Moving On

Where did the immigrants first set foot in America? That depended on where their ship was going. Most of those freight ships did business with the East Coast ports of New York, Philadelphia, Boston, and Baltimore, so that is where most European immigrants first landed. But a large number traveled on freighters bound for New Orleans. For them, that city was their introduction to America.

Many immigrants planned from the beginning to move on from the port where they landed. Just where they would move depended on a number of things. Those things included the city they arrived in, the amount of money in their pockets when they arrived, their skills, and especially, the locations where others of their nationality had already settled.

Some immigrants owned small farms in their homelands, which they managed to sell before leaving. That gave them money to buy farmland in America, preferably in a climate they were used to. So after arriving, they made their way to places where they could farm.

More than half the German immigrants who arrived during these years before the Civil War entered the United States through New Orleans. Many of them, too, came with enough money to buy farmland. Most made their way up the Mississippi River and carved out farms in Missouri, Ohio, Illinois, and Wisconsin.

This image shows Chinese immigrants in an area of San Francisco that became known as Chinatown. The first Chinese immigrants arrived in San Francisco in 1848, before the Civil War. Many cities in America have their very own Italian or Chinese sections.

Immigrants with special work skills often went where there was a demand for those skills. A Welsh coal miner, for example, would head for the coal mines of eastern Pennsylvania. Someone who had worked in one of the British textile factories would go to a town where cottons or woolens were being manufactured—usually in Massachusetts, New York, or Pennsylvania.

And of course, it was natural for immigrants to settle where relatives, friends, and others from their country were already living. Living among their own made their adjustment to America a bit easier.

Remaining in the Cities

A good number of immigrants who came in this wave of immigration in the 1830s, 1840s, and 1850s, though, remained in the cities where they landed. Does that seem surprising? After all, hadn't most of those people been farmers? And for them, wasn't the promise of America about plentiful land?

Well, yes—for most, but not all. About one in every five who arrived before the Civil War was a skilled worker who had lived in a town or a city in Europe.

They included cabinetmakers, tailors, carpenters, weavers, shoemakers, printers, and bookbinders. Those were still the days before machines replaced such skills in the United States. Skilled workers settled in American cities because that's where they could find customers for their services.

As for the other four-fifths who had made their living from the land, most were far too poor to buy a farm when they arrived. In fact, they were too poor even to travel beyond the cities where they landed. They had to find work quickly. Without skills, they had nothing to sell but their muscle power and their time. They took whatever work they could get, at whatever pay they were offered.

Cities had plenty of jobs that needed doing. There were streets to be swept, ships to be loaded and unloaded, stables to be cleaned, garbage and trash to be hauled, ditches to be dug, and heavy loads to be carried. In the 1850s, there were thousands of such jobs in New York City alone—and most of them were held by immigrants! Another kind of job open to immigrant women in the cities was domestic work—that is, working as a maid or a house cleaner.

Of all the immigrants, the Irish were the poorest. Many had worked on the land in Ireland and so did not have other specific skills. Irish men often hired themselves out to work on the construction of railroads, canals, and other projects in the West. (In later years, Chinese, Mexican, and Italian laborers provided the muscle power that built America's railroads, but in this earlier period, before the 1860s, such work was performed by the Irish.)

Some of the Irish who worked in the railroad gangs settled in railroad cities, such as Albany, Buffalo, Cleveland, and Chicago. These workers were the start of large Irish communities in those places.

But of course, it was not the Irish alone who filled America's cities. French Canadians moved into the cotton mill towns of New England, and large numbers of Germans settled in New York, Cincinnati, Milwaukee, and St. Louis. And there were English immigrants scattered among a number of America's growing cities.

Later, after the Civil War, Irish and Chinese immigrants worked together to build the Transcontinental Railroad.

Immigrant Life in the Cities

Living conditions for most immigrants in American cities were simply dreadful. In the 1850s, investigators did a study of the housing in New York City. Just read their description of one building, where seventy Irish immigrants lived:

This is a three-story building . . . over a stable where an express company's horses are kept. The dilapidation [run-down condition] of this entire building is extreme; its rickety floors shook under the tread, and portions of the wall, black and **mildewed**, were continually breaking off. . . . A poor woman who occupied an apartment on the second floor complained, "The ould [old] ceiling . . . is ould as meself, and it's full uv the dhrop it is," meaning, it was soaked with water that entered through the broken roof whenever it rained.

Most large American cities had immigrant neighborhoods with run-down houses. This image shows a tenement building in New York City. People lived crowded into small rooms in buildings that were in need of repair.

After such a rain, the investigators discovered, the upper floors of the **tenement** were completely flooded, and the people had "to move their drenched beds from spot to spot."

How crowded were they? "In one of the rooms of the front house, an apartment six feet by ten in

area, a widow lived with five children." Six people in a room the size of a large closet! One has to wonder what kind of American letter such a person would have written to family and friends back home in Ireland.

One area in New York City stands out most of all. It was a part of lower Manhattan known as the Five Points. The Five Points was so cramped, dangerous, and unhygienic that it became notorious. Charles Dickens and Abraham Lincoln visited the Five Points and spoke out about the conditions. The neighborhood, before the Civil War, was made up mostly of Irish immigrants. Later, Germans, Italians, European Jews, and African Americans lived there. It is said that out of this mix of cultures came the phenomenon of American tap dancing.

And yet, it is important to remember that while the lives of many immigrants were hard, that was not true for all. Those who came as skilled workers generally had fewer problems adjusting to life in America. They were soon paid as well as skilled workers born in America, and they were far better off than they had been in Europe. The same was true for the hundreds of thousands who took up farming—especially for those immigrants who were able to buy their own farmland. For such persons, America truly was a land of opportunity.

Those who struggled were mostly the poor and unskilled, who were crowded into cities, and who lived in dreadful conditions. However, despite these hardships, they believed they had one thing in America they had not had before—a future, for themselves and their children. That was why they scrimped and saved to bring over other family members to join them. Every time an immigrant purchased a ship ticket to send to a relative back home, he was casting a vote for America.

Chapter 3
The New Immigration

Millions Come In the fifty years before the Civil War, about five million immigrants entered the United States. Does that seem like a lot of people? It is. But that was just a taste of what was to come. During the fifty years after the war, about another 25 million immigrants entered the United States!

The Big Question
....

How would you compare the experiences of those who came to America as part of the "old wave of immigration" to the experiences of those who were part of the "new wave of immigration"?

Immigration continued to rise in the 1850s, and there was even immigration during the period of the Civil War in America. After the Civil War, immigration increased significantly. In 1882, three quarters of a million people reached America's shores.

The peaks and valleys on the graph on page 21 shows that immigration was not a steady stream. In some years there were many immigrants; in others there were fewer. This uneven flow of immigrants was caused by changing conditions in Europe and the United States. People were more likely to leave Europe when times were especially bad, and they were more likely to come to the United States when jobs were plentiful and the American economy was strong. So you see, "reading" this graph on immigration can also tell you something about the history of the American economy.

One reason for the huge increase in immigration to America was that crossing the Atlantic Ocean had become faster, safer, cheaper, and more comfortable.

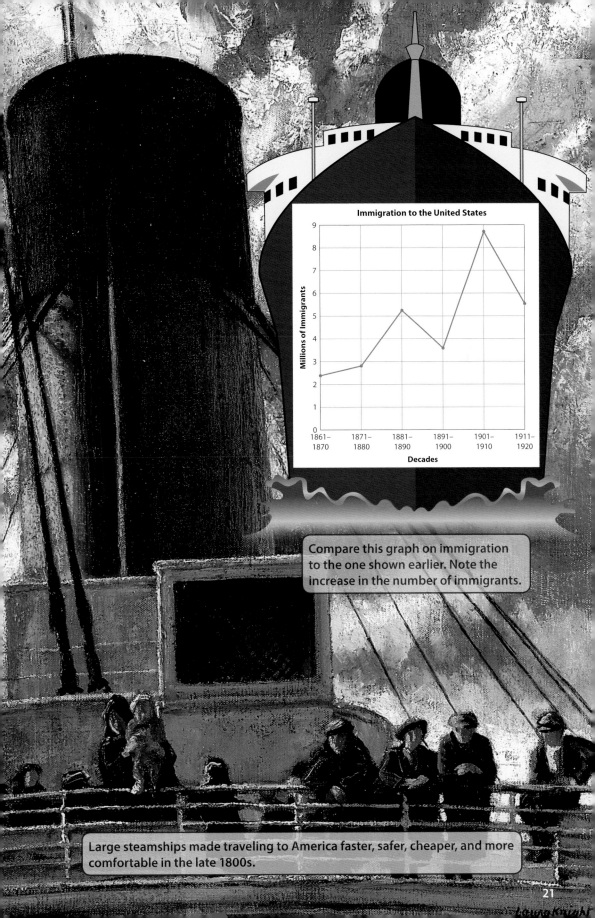

Immigration to the United States

Compare this graph on immigration to the one shown earlier. Note the increase in the number of immigrants.

Large steamships made traveling to America faster, safer, cheaper, and more comfortable in the late 1800s.

That was because large steamships had now replaced sailing vessels. Instead of six weeks, steamships made the crossing from England in six days—sometimes just five. The journey from more distant countries, like Greece and Italy, took less than two weeks. The cost of crossing the Atlantic was also much lower—$10 or $15, an amount that an immigrant laborer could earn in a few weeks in America.

Furthermore, immigrants could now travel on ships made for carrying passengers rather than freight. That meant that ocean crossings would not be nearly as uncomfortable as those of thirty or forty years earlier.

Where They Came From

Many of the immigrants of the 1860s, 1870s, and 1880s came from the same countries as earlier immigrants had come from—Germany, Great Britain, Ireland, as well as from the Scandinavian countries of Sweden, Denmark, and Norway. These countries are all located in the northern and western parts of Europe.

However, starting in the 1870s, immigrants began to arrive from the countries of southern and eastern Europe—countries such as Italy, Greece, Russia, Poland, and Austria-Hungary. Immigration from these countries has come to be called the New Immigration, while immigration from northern and western Europe is known as the Old Immigration. Maps tell the story of the Old and the New Immigration. Compare the information on the map titled "Old Immigration, 1820–1860" on page 5, with the map titled "New Immigration, 1870–1920" on page 23.

In addition to the Europeans, perhaps seventy thousand people came from Japan and another two hundred thousand from China. Thousands more moved across the borders from our neighbors, Canada and Mexico.

By the start of the 1900s, immigration to the United States reached new highs. Six times between 1900 and 1914, immigration exceeded one million people per year. By this time, most of the newcomers—in fact, 80 percent of them—were part of the New Immigration. That is, they were from the countries of southern and eastern Europe.

New Immigration, 1870–1920

Immigration to the United States changed after 1870. Many of the New Immigrants came from eastern or southern Europe.

Why They Came

Most of the New Immigrants came for pretty much the same reasons so many of the Old Immigrants did. These people were peasants—poor farming people. Most would have been happy to stay in their own countries if they could have made a living. But with population growing rapidly, there was not enough land to go around.

Once they got to America—the land of opportunity—the great majority of the New Immigrants wanted to stay and build new lives. But not all did. About one in every three who came to America during those years never intended to stay. Their main reason for coming to America was to earn enough money to buy land back home. Some went back and forth every year. As one of them said, "Doctor, we brought to America only our brains and our arms. Our hearts stayed there in the little house in the beautiful fields of our Italy." Such immigrants became known as "birds of passage."

For several groups of New Immigrants, there could be no thought of returning to their homelands. These were **persecuted** people. People who in their native lands were targeted simply because they spoke a different language, had different customs, or followed a religion that their government did not permit.

> **Vocabulary**
>
> **persecuted,** adj. treated cruelly or unfairly
>
> **pogrom,** n. an organized killing of a group of people; usually used to refer to attacks on Jews in Eastern Europe in the 1800s and early 1900s

Millions of Poles, Slovaks, Slovenes, and people of other nationalities lived under foreign rule. Often they weren't allowed to have newspapers or books in their own language, or to get very far in school or in work unless they gave up their language. In Russia, millions of Jews were regularly persecuted for their religious beliefs.

One of those Jews who fled Russia has given us a frightening picture of what it was like to experience a **pogrom**, or massacre. The Russian government

Many Jewish people had to flee Russia because they were oppressed and persecuted for their religious beliefs.

actually encouraged such attacks. In her autobiography, *The Promised Land*, this woman, Mary Antin, wrote:

> In Russian cities, and even more in the country districts, where Jewish families lived scattered, by special permission of the police, who were always changing their minds about letting them stay, the Gentiles [Christians] . . . would set out to kill the Jews. They attacked them with knives and clubs and scythes and axes, killed them or tortured them, and burned their homes.

For these immigrants, once they left Europe for America there was no turning back.

The Immigrant and the City

There was one more big difference between the Old Immigration and the New. Ask those who made up the Old Immigration what their dream of America had been before they arrived, and most would reply, "great open spaces and plenty of land for farming." Ask those who made up the New Immigration, and most would say, "great cities and well paid jobs in factories." The immigrants' image of America had changed because America itself had changed.

New Immigrants poured into cities in even greater numbers than did the Old Immigrants. The huge tides of immigration, both Old and New, changed the very makeup of America's large cities. Near the end of the 1800s, foreign-born people made up at least one-third of the population of such cities as New York, Chicago, and San Francisco. Indeed, together with their American-born children, they made up more than nine of every ten residents of Chicago, and about eight of every ten in Milwaukee, Detroit, New York, Cleveland, St. Louis, and San Francisco.

No city had a bigger variety of immigrants, and more of each group, than New York around 1900.

- More Italians lived in New York than in any city in Italy except its capital, Rome.
- More Greeks lived in New York than in any city in Greece except its capital, Athens.
- More Germans lived in New York than in any city in Germany except its capital, Berlin.
- More Irish lived in New York than in any city in Ireland except its capital, Dublin.
- More Jews lived in New York than in any city anywhere in the world.

A Foreign Flavor

With numbers such as these, the New Immigrants gave American cities a foreign flavor. Just as was the case in the immigration of the 1840s and 1850s, members of each immigrant group chose to live near people who were the same as them. As you have already discovered, many immigrants wanted to be with people who spoke their language, practiced their religion, and shared their customs. So in most cities there were Italian neighborhoods, Jewish neighborhoods, and Polish neighborhoods, as well as German, Irish, and Greek. People from China had been arriving in America since the days of the California Gold Rush. Many were later hired to build the Central Pacific Railroad in the 1860s. Later, the Chinese spread throughout the West, settling down in both large and small cities.

Few Japanese immigrants arrived in North America much before the end of the 1800s. Eventually, about seventy thousand came. Most took up farming and fishing, but a number opened small shops in some of the cities in the states of Washington and California.

As you have discovered, the railroads of America were largely built by immigrants. After the Civil War, Chinese labor was a huge factor in making this happen.

Making a living in the city was not easy for the New Immigrants. Most had no skills and spoke no English. Usually, they wound up with the hardest jobs, the longest hours, and the lowest pay. And often they met with **discrimination**. Here, for example, are the daily wages offered in a newspaper advertisement for workers on a construction project in New York in 1895:

> Common labor, white, $1.30 to $1.50 a day
>
> Common labor, black, $1.25 to $1.40 a day
>
> Common labor, Italian, $1.15 to $1.25 a day

The New Immigrants worked in textile factories, steel mills, and **meatpacking plants**. They made cigars in crowded workshops or sometimes in their own homes. They did housework for others, worked in **canneries**, and labored in the garment industry. Often, everyone in the family, including young children, had to work to earn enough to live on.

Immigrants also helped build the city itself. Back in Europe, many of the immigrants had heard it said that "in America, the streets are paved with gold." As someone later wrote, though, when they arrived in the United States, they quickly learned three things about that saying: "First, that the streets were not paved with gold; second, that the streets were not paved at all; and third, that they [the immigrants] were expected to pave them." And they did. They, along with the descendants of enslaved African Americans, built the streets, the bridges, and the water and sewer systems that made the modern city possible.

Hard as life may have been for them, however, these new Americans knew they were often far better off than they had been in their native lands. In time, many learned new skills and improved their earnings. They were able to afford better housing than the rundown apartment buildings where they had started life in America. Most important, with the help of free public schools, their children had a future. Within one generation, or sometimes two, many of those children were entering the fields of medicine, education, business, law, and a hundred other occupations.

Immigrant children often started working at a young age to help support the family.

This immigrant family worked together to make clothing. They were paid for each piece they produced.

Chapter 4
An Uncertain Welcome

Happy Birthday, America! Birthdays are customary occasions for gift giving, certainly. But the birthday gift the American people were given on July 4, 1884, was, to say the least, unusual. It was a gigantic statue of a woman, weighing 225 tons and standing 151 feet high— about as tall as a fifteen-story building.

The Big Question

What were the different reactions to the "sudden flood" of particular groups of immigrants?

In one hand, the statue held high a great torch. In the other, she held a tablet bearing the date of the Declaration of Independence. This statue was a gift from the people of France. It was designed and built in France by a young sculptor named Frédéric-Auguste Bartholdi, and it was paid for by contributions from thousands of ordinary French people. They intended this gift to celebrate the friendship of the French and the Americans during the American Revolution. They also intended it to express their own belief in the idea of liberty. The name that Bartholdi gave to his statue was *Liberty Enlightening the World*. You know it by another name: the Statue of Liberty.

Newcomers to the United States, who arrived in New York, often gathered at the ship's railing to gaze at the Statue of Liberty—the symbol of liberty and freedom for all.

The Statue of Liberty, a gift from France, stands on a small island in New York Harbor.

Bartholdi's work was so huge that it had to be shipped in pieces from France in 214 wooden crates. This gift actually arrived in New York in 1885, and the following year was assembled on a tiny island in New York Harbor. There it remains to this day, a **symbol** of liberty that thrills Americans and foreign visitors alike.

A Symbol of Welcome

Within a very short time, however, the Statue of Liberty became a symbol of something else, too. In the 1800s, most immigrants entered America through the port of New York. As their ship entered the harbor, passengers rushed to the railing to get a good view of Lady Liberty, as some called it. For them, the Statue of Liberty, standing on its island in the middle of New York Harbor, was the symbol of America's welcome to the newcomers.

Immigrants were not alone in thinking of the statue in this way. Emma Lazarus was a young poet whose family had come to this land more than two centuries earlier. Lazarus was deeply disturbed by the reports of the pogroms taking place in Russia. More than ever, she appreciated the liberty and the religious freedom people enjoyed in America. She wrote a poem called, "The New **Colossus**" to express what the Statue of Liberty meant to her.

Emma Lazarus's poem is only fourteen lines long, but it is one of the best known of all poems written by an American. After Lazarus died, the last five lines of the poem were carved into the base of the Statue of Liberty. If you ever visit the statue, you will see them there:

> Give me your tired, your poor,
>
> Your huddled masses yearning to breathe free,
>
> The wretched refuse of your teeming shore.
>
> Send these, the homeless, tempest-tost to me,
>
> I lift my lamp beside the golden door!

Imagine what this family was feeling as they arrived in the United States. Many immigrants had little money and could not speak English.

Ellis Island

Most immigrants who arrived after 1892 first set foot on American soil at another island in New York Harbor called Ellis Island. There the government had built a new receiving station that could handle five thousand people a day.

When that proved too small, the facility was enlarged to handle up to fifteen thousand immigrants a day. Even then, there were some days when it was overflowing! All together, sixteen million people passed through Ellis Island, the great bulk of them in the first thirty years of its existence. (It was closed in 1954.)

Can you imagine what the immigrant felt on arriving at Ellis Island? Excitement? Oh yes. America at last—the very first step on American land! But uncertainty and fear, too. Most worrisome was the physical examination. Immigrants knew that those who failed to pass would be sent back to their homeland. The illness of a single child in a large family could mean a wrenching decision: Should they all return to where they came from? Or should one parent go back with the sick child and the other remain in America with the rest, hoping and praying for an early reunion? Only a small minority were turned back, but you can understand why, for some, Ellis Island became known as the Island of Tears.

Immigrants feared the medical examination just in case they were refused entry into the United States.

Ellis Island was an immigrant processing center in New York Harbor. Today, it is a museum and an immigration research center.

After the physical examination came another examination. Immigration inspectors would ask each immigrant's name. If the official wasn't sure how to spell a name, he would give the immigrant a simpler, more English-sounding name. For example, the name Wallenchinsky might be written down as "Wallace." There were other questions, too: Where are you from? Any relatives in America? Why are you coming? Where will you live? Do you have a job waiting for you? There were no wrong answers, but even so, the process could be nerve-racking and bewildering. When it was all over, the immigrants would be on their way to their new life.

The Rise of Nativism

Emma Lazarus's poem of welcome at the base of the Statue of Liberty spoke for many Americans, but not for all. You see, even from the earliest days of our country's history, Americans were of two minds about immigration. On the one hand, Americans favored immigration because immigrants helped settle the land and build up the country. But on the other hand—and often at the very same time—immigrants who were different from themselves in nationality, language, customs, or religion troubled them.

Those mixed feelings have continued right on to the present. For most of our history, the positive feelings about immigration have outweighed the negative. "Let the immigrants come," many people have said. "The more the better. Let them enjoy the blessings of liberty as they help build our land." Americans were confident that in one or two generations, the newcomers would become Americans like themselves.

There have been times in the past, though, when a *large* number of Americans thought differently. They feared that immigrants were changing America—and changing it for the worse. They were no longer confident that these newcomers would become American quickly, or that they would become American at all. When Americans felt that way, they were more ready to listen to those who would take down the welcome signs. Such strong anti-immigrant feeling is called **nativism**.

The 1850s was one time when nativism was on the rise. The main objection **nativists** raised against the immigrants then entering America was their religion. Many were Catholics from Ireland and from Germany. To some Protestants, this sudden flood of Catholics seemed like a threat to American culture. They feared the influence of Catholic Church leaders, such as bishops, who might be tempted to influence Catholics when it came to voting. They called for laws to end, or at least sharply limit, further immigration. Congress did not pass any such laws, but as the Civil War approached, immigration declined on its own.

> ## Vocabulary
>
> **nativism,** n. a policy of giving preference to people who are from a specific country, or who already live in a country, rather than to immigrants
>
> **nativist,** n. a person who has strong feelings against immigrants and wants to ban further immigration

Some nativists formed a movement that was somewhat jokingly given the name the Know Nothing movement. Members of the movement were for the most part anti-Catholic and anti-immigrant. The movement got its name because at first it was basically a secret society, and those involved claimed that they knew nothing about it. The Know Nothing movement did go on to become a political party known as the American Party—though it did not last for very long.

By the time immigration rose once again after the Civil War, the mood of the country had changed back to one of welcome. There was, however, one great exception. In the American West, a current of nativism continued to run

The *American Patriot* newspaper was published specifically to attack Catholic, and in particular, Irish immigrants. This is an example of the front page of an 1852 edition.

strong against Chinese immigrants. They were ridiculed and discriminated against wherever they went. They were also victims of robbery, beatings, and even murder, and those responsible were rarely punished.

The U.S. Congress passed two laws that reflected this anti-Chinese sentiment. The first, in 1870, was designed to make it impossible for any Chinese immigrant, even one who had lived in the United States for years, to become an American citizen. The second, in 1882, put an end to all Chinese immigration into the United States. This law was known as the Chinese Exclusion Act. It remained an American law for more than sixty years.

On the West Coast, Angel Island, in San Francisco Bay, was an immigration station much like Ellis Island. Here, thousands of Chinese and Japanese immigrants were detained under harsh conditions.

Here you can see a Japanese immigrant mother and her child.

The Return of Nativism

The welcoming of European immigrants, however, continued into the 1880s. And then—ironically, at about the time the Statue of Liberty was placed on its pedestal in New York Harbor—the mood of America changed once more. By the 1890s, nativism had once again flared up.

The target of this flare-up was the New Immigration—immigrants from southern and eastern Europe. "These people are too different," cried nativists. "They are not like us. They speak strange languages, wear strange clothing, and they follow strange customs. Most are either Catholic, Jewish, or Greek or Russian Orthodox in religion. Many come from lands that have never known democracy.

They have no experience with **representative government** and no desire for it. They will never fit in. They don't even want to fit in. They will ruin America."

All of us today know that these New Immigrants became as American as the Old Immigrants. We know that the United States has benefited greatly from their contributions. But nativists presented these claims in articles and speeches as though they were proven facts. Worse still, many of their readers and listeners believed them.

The immigrants who came as part of the wave of New Immigration contributed greatly to the United States. They brought knowledge, skills, and a desire to work hard to succeed.

Labor leaders tended to be particularly worried about immigration. They feared that the new immigrants would work for lower wages, leaving native-born workers unemployed. Here is how one congressman sympathetic to such labor leaders summed up the case against immigrants:

> Immigrants work for wages upon which American workingmen cannot live. The evidence abundantly shows that they habitually live in **shanties**; that they eat the

Vocabulary

"representative government," (phrase) a government in which citizens elect people to rule for them; a republic

shanty, n. a small, simple wood building

rudest food; that they do not have even the most common sanitary appliances; that they expose themselves to all the diseases that are generated by filth. The American workingman cannot support churches and decently clothe his children and send them to school and enjoy any of the comforts of civilization, so long as he must come into this degrading competition.

With nativism on the rise, there were again demands that the government limit the number who entered the United States. Once again, however, no action was taken, and soon nativist sentiment died down. In fact, in the twenty or so years that followed, our country received more immigrants than in any similar period before.

Nativism, however, had not had its last say. In the 1920s, the United States adopted its first major laws to limit immigration. But that is a story for another time.

Chapter 5
Becoming American

Melting Pot In 1909, a British author named Israel Zangwill wrote a play called *The Melting Pot* about the immigrant experience in the United States. At one point, as though welcoming new arrivals to America, Zangwill has one of his characters say:

The Big Question

Why do you think "becoming an American" was easier for those who were born in America to immigrants, than for those who had moved to America from the country of their birth?

America is God's **crucible**, the great Melting Pot where all the races of Europe are melting and re-forming. Here you stand, good folk, think I, when I see you at Ellis Island, here you stand, in your fifty groups, with your fifty languages and histories, and your fifty blood hatreds and rivalries. But you won't be long like that, brothers, for these are the fires of God you come to—these are the fires of God. A fig for your feuds and vendettas! German and Frenchmen, Irishmen and Englishmen, Jews and Russians, into the Crucible with you all! God is making the American!

Vocabulary

crucible, n. a container used for melting substances at a very high heat

When Zangwill's play opened in Washington, D.C., on October 5, 1909, President Theodore Roosevelt went to see it. Later the president wrote to Zangwill and told him, "That particular play I shall always count among the very strong and real influences upon my thought and my life."

Israel Zangwill was the son of Russian and Jewish immigrants who had settled in England. Zangwill wrote about the poor, the homeless, and the oppressed.

Ever since then, Zangwill's image of a melting pot has been used by many to describe the process by which immigrants become American—mixing together socially, perhaps marrying one another, or maybe just living side by side. You will find on American coins the motto *e pluribus unum*, which is Latin for "out of many, one." That refers to the creation of a single nation out of many states under the American Constitution. But the melting pot image seemed to give the motto a new meaning. Out of many different peoples, one people: the American people.

Was Israel Zangwill correct? Is that what happens? That question is a difficult one, and not everyone would answer it the same way. We can say this much for sure: If the image of a melting pot does fairly describe how immigrant peoples become Americans, then for most of these peoples the melting process took a long time—often several generations—to work. And it was rarely easy.

The First Generation

A great many of the new arrivals—the first-generation Americans—were not in a hurry to "become American." You'll remember that usually the members of each group lived together in neighborhoods, where they could be with people from their country of origin. They at first felt most comfortable around people who came not only from their own country but sometimes even from their own village. These were people they could depend on to help them make their way in the strange new world.

As much as possible, first-generation Americans tried to recreate the familiar ways of their old life. First and foremost was their religious life. Every immigrant group since the Pilgrims and the Puritans had made their religion a priority. From their small wages, they scraped together money to build their own church or **synagogue**. There, with others who spoke the same language, they shared religious customs and holidays and taught their children the religious beliefs of their own people. There also, they hoped their sons and daughters

> **Vocabulary**
>
> **synagogue,** n. a Jewish house of worship

44

In New York City, just as in other cities across America, new immigrants were attracted to neighborhoods where people from their own country lived. This photograph shows immigrants in the Lower East Side of New York City in the early 1900s.

would meet and marry their own kind. They founded their own cemeteries, for it was important that they not be buried among strangers. In time, they also set up their own nursing homes, orphanages, and hospitals.

The foreign language newspaper was another important part of immigrant life. In 1900, there were more than one thousand such newspapers in the United States, and in dozens of languages. Through these newspapers, immigrants kept up with news of the old villages back home, as well as the things happening in their new country. The news of marriages, births, deaths, and activities in their own immigrant communities was of particular interest. Such news was not likely to be carried in the city's English-language newspapers.

Did living in their own neighborhoods and reading newspapers in their own language slow down the process of becoming American? Or did these things help by forming a bridge to American life that immigrants could cross at their own pace? Probably both. Although many immigrants did learn to speak and read English, there were those who never did. And being able to read a newspaper in their own language probably made it less necessary for them to do so. Yet, as they experienced life in this new world and learned more of American ways—often by reading those very newspapers—they, too, day by day and year by year, were becoming American.

Even so, around the turn of the century there were some Americans who were concerned that immigrants were moving too slowly across the bridge from being a foreigner to becoming American. They created special programs intended to speed the immigrants' journey. These programs were called Americanization programs. Clubs, businesses, and various organizations printed millions of pamphlets to teach immigrants about American government and society. Some churches, volunteer groups, and city governments ran evening schools and other programs where immigrants could learn English.

These efforts to bring the newcomers into the mainstream of American life were well intended. There was probably much good in them. But too often, those who ran them were not sensitive to the feelings of the people on the receiving end. As one immigrant remembered in later years, this was their message:

> Forget your native land, forget your mother tongue, do away in a day with your inherited customs, put from you as a cloak all that inheritance and early environment made you, and become in a day an American.

They seemed to be saying, recalled this immigrant, "Either become an American citizen or get out." Most immigrants found it was not that easy to do the one, and they desperately did not want to do the other.

The Second Generation

It was the second generation—the American-born children of the immigrants—who succeeded in crossing the bridge to the American side much more successfully. More than anything else it was the American public school that helped them make that crossing. In those schools, the children of the immigrants learned to speak and write English. American-born teachers taught them about American history and American government; and all the while, in school and out, these second-generation Americans were becoming accustomed to American ways, tastes, habits, dress, and beliefs that touched on every part of their lives.

As these children became Americans, differences often arose between them and their immigrant parents. Many parents wanted to hold on to their traditional views of family life: the proper relationship of wife to husband, of child to parent, of young to old. To them, America seemed to be teaching their

In schools across America, the children of immigrants learned a new language and all about their new country. Here you can see the children of Italian immigrants at school in New York City in 1910.

children different lessons and to be encouraging their children to throw away a valuable heritage. The children, speaking one language at home and another at school, often saw their parents as simply old-fashioned, blocking their own way to being accepted as American.

Years later, one of these second-generation Americans recalled his feelings as he was growing up this way:

> My contemporaries [people his own age] had labeled me Italian. . . . I didn't want to be Italian. Or Swedish. Or Irish. Or anything "different." Like countless bewildered young people before me—and to come—I just wanted to be myself. "Why can't I just be Joe?" I thought.

The Third Generation

It was usually the third-generation—the grandchildren of the immigrants—who finally felt fully, comfortably American. By then, many had moved away from the old immigrant neighborhoods, and most of the foreign language newspapers no longer existed. Few of the third generation still spoke the language of the old country. Few were still torn between the ways of the old world and the ways of the new. Few asked themselves, "Why can't I just be Joe?" They knew that they already were "just Joe." If they chose to call themselves Italian or Irish or Swedish or anything else, that was their choice. They knew that whatever other label they might use, they were American.

New Americans

Most first-generation immigrants had the opportunity to become American citizens by being **naturalized**. This meant, and still does, that after fulfilling the legal requirements, they could become full-fledged Americans with full voting rights. Future generations, born in the

Vocabulary

naturalize, v. to allow someone from another country to become a citizen

United States, would automatically be citizens. This is still true, though today, would-be Americans must pass a required civics and American history test.

Today the phrase *melting pot* in many ways has been replaced by the word *mosaic*—something that is made from many different shapes, sizes, colors, and parts. So perhaps we can say that the history of America resembles the creation of a mosaic. Would you agree?

At the naturalization ceremony, which all new citizens take part in, they take the Oath of Allegiance.

Glossary

B

blight, n. a disease that causes plants to dry up and die (7)

C

cannery, n. a factory where food is packaged in cans (28)

colossus, n. a statue that is larger than life-size (32)

crucible, n. a container used for melting substances at a very high heat (42)

D

descendant, n. someone who is related to a person or group of people who lived in the past (2)

discrimination, n. unfair treatment of a person or group because of beliefs about that group of people (28)

E

economic, adj. relating to the management of money and resources to produce, buy, and sell goods and services (6)

emigration, n. the act of leaving one country to settle permanently in another (4)

F

freight, n. shipped goods; cargo (14)

I

immigration, n. the act of coming to live permanently in a new country (2)

M

"meatpacking plant," (phrase) a factory where livestock are killed and their meat is processed, packaged, and distributed (28)

mildewed, adj. affected by a fungus that grows in damp conditions (17)

N

nativism, n. a policy of giving preference to people who are from a specific country, or who already live in a country, rather than to immigrants (36)

nativist, n. a person who has strong feelings against immigrants and wants to ban further immigration (36)

naturalize, v. to allow someone from another country to become a citizen (48)

P

persecuted, adj. treated cruelly or unfairly (24)

pogrom, n. an organized killing of a group of people; usually used to refer to attacks on Jews in Eastern Europe in the 1800s and early 1900s (24)

R

"representative government," (phrase) a government in which citizens elect people to rule for them; a republic (40)

S

shanty, n. a small, simple wood building (40)

symbol, n. an object or picture that stands for something else (32)

synagogue, n. a Jewish house of worship (44)

T

tenement, n. an apartment building, often overcrowded and in need of repairs, usually in a city slum (19)

V

vulnerable, adj. lacking protection; likely to be hurt physically or emotionally; weak (6)

Industrialization and Urbanization in America

Table of Contents

Reader

Core Knowledge History and Geography™

Chapter 1
The Industrial Giant

Rich and Poor In 1848, thirteen-year-old Andrew Carnegie arrived in the United States from Scotland, along with his younger brother, his mother, and his father, who was an unemployed **weaver**. Landing in New York, the Carnegies continued on to Pittsburgh, Pennsylvania, where they had relatives.

The Big Question

How did America transform from an agricultural nation into an industrial giant?

Vocabulary

weaver, n. a person who makes fabric by weaving threads or yarn together

Having come with little money in their pockets, the Carnegies needed to find work quickly—not only for the mother and father, but for young Andrew as well.

Andrew's first job was as a bobbin boy in a mill that spun cotton into thread. When the bobbins, or spools, on the spinning machines filled up with thread, Andrew replaced them with empty ones. The job did not call for much skill, and it paid just $1.20 a week. That came to twenty cents a day, six days a week, working from sunrise to sunset. It was not much, but it was an important addition to his parents' small income.

In this photograph you can see a bobbin boy replacing full bobbins with empty ones. The boy in the photograph is not Andrew Carnegie, but as a thirteen-year-old, Carnegie did the very same job.

After a number of such simple and low-wage jobs, Andrew taught himself to become a **telegraph** operator. In the evenings, he went to school to learn bookkeeping—how to keep records of incoming and outgoing money transactions in a business. On his own, he read the important English, Scottish, and American writers of the day.

When he was seventeen, Andrew caught the eye of Thomas A. Scott, an official at the Pennsylvania Railroad Company. Scott hired Andrew as his personal telegraph operator and secretary, starting him at $35 a week, a large salary in those days and more than Carnegie ever imagined he would earn.

In the late 1800s, Andrew Carnegie became one of the richest men in the world.

As Scott moved up the company ladder, Andrew moved with him, taking on greater responsibilities and earning more money.

Carnegie saved and became a wise **investor**. By the age of thirty-three his income from his salary and investments was $50,000 a year (that would be more than a half million dollars a year today). Soon after, he entered into business for himself,

and his wealth increased steadily. By the year 1883, Andrew Carnegie was a multimillionaire.

In that same year, a committee of the U.S. Senate held hearings to learn about working conditions in America's factories. One of the people who testified was thirty-year-old Thomas O'Donnell. Like Carnegie, O'Donnell had come to America as a poor boy. Also like Carnegie, he had immediately gone to work in a **textile** factory. But that is where the similarities ended. Life had turned out quite differently for Tom O'Donnell than it had for Andrew Carnegie, as O'Donnell's answers to the senators' questions made clear:

Q: Are you a married man?

A: Yes, sir; I am a married man; have a wife and two children. I am not very well educated. I went to work when I was young, and have been working ever since in the cotton business; went to work when I was about eight or nine years old . . . .

Q: How much work have you had within a year?

A: . . . . About fifteen weeks' work . . . .

Q: That would be somewhere around $133 [wages for the year]?

A: Yes, sir.

Q: To support yourself and wife and two children?

A: Yes, sir.

Q: Do you mean that yourself and wife and two children have had nothing but that for all this time?

A: That is all. I got a couple dollars' worth of coal last winter, and the wood I picked up myself. I goes around with a shovel and picks up clams [pieces of coal] and wood . . . .

Q: You have not any [work] now, you say?

A: No, sir . . . .

Q: What have the children got on in the way of clothing?

A: . . . . One has one shoe on, a very poor one, and a slipper, that was picked up somewhere. The other has two odd shoes on, one with the heel out. He has got cold and is sickly now.

Both Andrew Carnegie's enormous wealth and the O'Donnell family's daily struggle to survive were products of a great change that swept across America in the late 1800s. (You will learn more about Andrew Carnegie later.) That change goes by the name of *industrialization*—the production of goods by machines in large factories, rather than by hand.

Laying the Foundations

Great changes in human history do not happen overnight. The shift from an agricultural to an industrial society in the United States was no exception. The first tiny steps in this change occurred when George Washington was still president of the United States. Back then, nearly all Americans made everything by hand in their own homes, just as their grandparents had done. Take clothing, for example: To make a cotton or wool shirt, a woman first spun raw cotton or wool into thread on a spinning wheel. She then wove this thread into cloth on a loom. On a good day, a woman could produce a yard or so of cloth. Finally, she cut and sewed the cloth into a shirt.

In Great Britain, however, several people had already invented machines that could spin cotton into thread. Others had invented machines that could

For hundreds of years, women and children worked at home spinning cotton or wool into thread to make cloth.

weave cotton thread and wool yarn into cloth. Driven by water power and housed in new factory buildings, these machines could produce not one but hundreds of yards of cloth a day.

British merchants were soon selling British textiles all over the world, bringing riches to their country. To keep this advantage for their own **manufacturers**, the British government prohibited anyone from selling a spinning or weaving machine to another country, or taking plans for making one out of Great Britain.

> **Vocabulary**
>
> **manufacturer,** n. a person or company that makes or produces an item to be sold

No one who had even worked in a cotton mill was allowed to leave the country.

In the end, these efforts at secrecy failed. In 1789—the year Washington became our first president—Samuel Slater, a twenty-one-year-old worker in an English cotton mill, saw an advertisement in a newspaper. Several American businessmen were offering a handsome reward to anyone who could build a spinning machine for them. Slater, who had worked in an English cotton mill since the age of fourteen, knew the spinning machine inside and out.

Government officials, of course, were ready to stop any person from taking plans for making such a machine out of Great Britain. The law, however, did not protect against Slater's excellent memory. In 1789, Slater, disguised as

The first cotton mill in America (shown here) was established by Samuel Slater and two partners on the Blackstone River in Pawtucket, Rhode Island.

a farmer, boarded a ship bound for the United States. He was going there to seek his fortune, the plans for building a spinning machine fixed firmly in his head.

A little more than a year later, in 1791, in Pawtucket, Rhode Island, Slater and two American partners opened the first cotton-**spinning mill** in the United States. In the next two decades, dozens of other spinning mills sprang up in New England, where fast-flowing streams and rivers provided the power to run the machines.

From Mills to Factories

These early mills made only cotton thread, not cloth. That still had to be made the old way, by women weaving on their handlooms (a weaving device operated by hand), at home. A trip to Great Britain in 1810 by a Boston merchant named Francis Lowell changed that. Visiting a weaving factory, Lowell quickly grasped the principles on which the power looms worked. Back home, he persuaded several wealthy Boston friends to join him in building a factory that would do even more. In 1814, the Waltham Associates, as they were called, opened their factory in the town of Waltham, Massachusetts, not far from Boston. There, under one roof, machines spun cotton into thread, workers dyed the thread, and other machines wove it into finished cloth. Lowell and his friends soon built more factories nearby, as did other investors.

With the opening of these mills, the factory system arrived in America. By the 1820s and 1830s, factories were producing other goods as well. There were mills that turned wheat into flour and others that turned trees into lumber. Factories did not depend on machines alone, however. There were factories in which people worked to make products by hand. In some cities in the Northeast, workers turned out shoes, clocks, kitchen pots and pans,

In this factory, thread was processed so it could be used to make lace.

and many other goods, in hundreds of such bustling workshops. By the time young Andrew Carnegie arrived in America in 1848, the foundations of an industrial society were already in place.

By 1848, although some factories and workshops were quite large, most employed fewer than twenty workers. Nearly half employed fewer than ten. Most workers still produced goods with hand tools like those their grandfathers had used. In addition, the majority of Americans still made their living by farming.

After the Civil War, however, the United States entered a period of dizzying industrial growth. Machine-made goods, everything from telephones to toys, poured out of America's new factories. The United States overtook

Great Britain as the world's largest producer of manufactured goods, and by 1900, American production was greater than that of Great Britain and France combined. In that year, more than five million people worked in America's factories. Another million worked on its railroads, and almost a million more labored in its mines.

The sweeping changes that took place in the last half of the 1800s can be summed up in two sentences: In 1850, the United States was mainly an agricultural nation. By 1900, it had become an industrial giant.

In the chapters that follow, you will read about how this industrial growth came about.

Chapter 2
Railroads

Growth of the Railroads Nothing was more important to America's industrial growth than railroads. Americans had been building railroads since the early 1830s. By the start of the Civil War in 1861, there were already more than thirty thousand miles of railroad track in the United States.

The Big Question

How did the development and expansion of railroads help grow the American economy?

That sounds like a lot of miles of track, and it was. However, for two reasons, it did not really add up to a national system of transportation. First, two-thirds of the thirty thousand miles of track were in the Northeast and Midwest. The South had most of the rest; the mountains and open spaces of the far West had almost none.

Second, those thirty thousand miles of track were owned by several hundred small companies, many of them with lines only forty or fifty miles long. An average railroad line ran for only about one hundred miles. Each company decided for itself how far apart to set its tracks. The space between tracks is called the *gauge* (/gayj/). You can guess what that meant: railroad cars made for one company would not necessarily fit on the rails of the others.

If you were shipping goods to a place several hundred miles away, this is what had to happen: First the goods were loaded onto a train and carried to the end of that railroad company's track, perhaps a hundred miles, or less. Then the

The Mohawk & Hudson Railroad ran the first steam railroad passenger train in America. It was made up of a steam engine with a railroad car carrying fuel, and passenger cars that looked like stagecoaches.

goods were unloaded, carried across town on wagons, and loaded onto the next company's train for the next hundred or so miles. That might be done multiple times before the goods reached their destination, adding greatly to shipping costs and time. For example, goods sent between New York and Chicago, a distance of about a thousand miles, had to be transferred fourteen different times along the way. It took two to three weeks for a shipment to arrive at its destination.

The thirty-five years between the end of the Civil War and the turn of the century saw the creation of a truly national railroad system in America. Year after year, railroad companies built thousands of miles of new track. The most spectacular construction took place in the West, where the great **transcontinental** lines were built. To encourage railroad companies to build lines across mountains and through what was considered to be the "unsettled plains" of that region, the **federal government** provided "free land" and loans of money. As you know, this unsettled land had once belonged to Native Americans.

Even more new track was laid in the settled parts of the country—the East, Midwest, and South. In these areas, it was often the state governments that aided the railroad companies with gifts of land. Local governments also frequently offered money to persuade companies to build lines through their towns.

Even with all of this government help, it was private investors in the railroad companies who put up the money to build most of the track miles. And what a record of building they achieved. By 1900, the United States had nearly two hundred thousand miles of track, more than all the countries of Europe combined. Railroads reached into every corner of this vast nation.

This photograph shows the celebration of the completion of the Transcontinental Railroad at Promontory Point in Utah. The Transcontinental Railroad was completed on May 10, 1869, when the Central Pacific Railroad coming from Sacramento, and the Union Pacific Railroad coming from Chicago, connected.

Cornelius Vanderbilt

During these same years, many of those small, separate railroad lines were combined into large networks. Cornelius Vanderbilt was a leader in this network building. Vanderbilt had already made a fortune in shipping before he entered the railroad business. Starting in the 1850s, he bought one small line after another on the route between New York City and Chicago. He converted all the track to the same gauge and added track to connect them. After that was done, the trip between those two cities could be made in less than a day, and without ever changing trains.

Cornelius Vanderbilt

Vanderbilt called his railroad system the New York Central. By the 1870s, the New York Central linked much of New York, Pennsylvania, Ohio, Indiana, and Illinois. At the same time, Tom Scott (the man who started Andrew Carnegie on his way to wealth) and others were connecting Pennsylvania, Missouri, and Illinois in a single network called the Pennsylvania Railroad.

Meanwhile, railroad companies agreed to adopt a standard gauge of forty-eight inches. By 1886, all but thirteen thousand miles of railroad track, mostly in the South, were set at that width. On May 30, 1886, railroad service in the South was suspended so that the thirteen thousand miles of track could be changed to the standard gauge. Incredibly, the work was completed in a single day!

Railroads and Growth

Just how did railroads contribute to the growth of industrial society? First, building, running, and maintaining the railroads created a huge demand for certain products. Take lumber, for example. Building railroads consumed huge amounts of timber for bridges, wagons, fuel, telegraph poles, and especially for railroad ties. Every mile of track required two thousand wooden ties, made from two hundred trees. By 1890, when ten miles of new track were being added every day, that meant two thousand trees were required each day. In addition, railroad workers needed timber to build railroad bridges, carriages, and the telegraph poles they erected every hundred feet along the track. Whole forests were cut down to satisfy the seemingly endless demand of the railroad builders. That meant a rapid growth for the lumber industry.

There was a similar demand for steel and coal. In 1880, three-fourths of all the steel produced in the United States was used to make steel rails. Still more steel was needed to manufacture engines and cars for the railroads. At the same time, thousands of **tons** of coal were needed each year to power the railroads' steam engines. All this contributed significantly to the growth of these and

> **Vocabulary**
>
> **ton,** n. a unit of weight equal to two thousand pounds

other industries in the United States. It created hundreds of thousands of jobs as well.

Railroads provided many different kinds of jobs: clearing land and laying track; building railroad engines and cars; running the railroad; not to mention all the industries that supplied materials to the railroads. In 1900, a million people worked on America's railroads.

In addition to providing jobs, railroads aided the growth of **industrialism** by swiftly and cheaply carrying raw materials to factories, and transporting manufactured goods to distant markets. It was this efficient transportation that made large-scale industrial production possible.

> ## Vocabulary
>
> **industrialism,** n.
> the organization of society around an economy based on the use of machines and factories

Pennsylvania was a center for steel production in the 1900s. Here you can see a steel production factory in Johnstown, Pennsylvania.

How Railroads Changed Business

It is worth taking a moment to do some simple math to see how railroads changed business. Let's say that in the days before railroads, there are two towns one hundred miles apart—we will call them Springfield and Pleasantville. In each town there is a manufacturer of iron stoves. The Springfield Stove Company sells its stoves for $50; the Pleasantville Stove Company, which is more efficient, sells a stove of equal quality for $40. Which iron stove will the people in each town buy?

Obviously, the people in Pleasantville will buy the stove made in their own town. It is as good as the one made in Springfield, and it costs $10 less. What about the people in Springfield? You might think those people would also buy the cheaper stove from the Pleasantville Stove Company for the same reason Pleasantville residents did. And they would, except for one thing—the cost of transportation. Remember, the towns are one hundred miles apart. Let's say the cost of shipping an iron stove by horse-drawn wagon—before the railroads were built—was $1 a mile. For one hundred miles, that comes to $100. People in Springfield must add that $100 to the price of the Pleasantville Company's $40 stove. $140 for a stove? Out of the question. People in Springfield will stick with the $50 stove made in their own town.

So both the Springfield and the Pleasantville stove companies will continue to make stoves. Because of the high cost of transportation, each company's market—that is, the area in which each company can hope to sell its stoves—will remain small. And both companies will therefore remain small.

Now let's see what happens after the railroad with its lower transportation costs connects Springfield and Pleasantville. That iron stove can now be shipped for only about a nickel a mile. Which stove will those Springfield residents buy now? Do the math: The Pleasantville company can now ship its $40 stove to Springfield for just five cents per mile times one hundred miles. It will now cost Springfield stove customers just $45, $5 less than the stove made in their own town.

Springfield residents will now buy the Pleasantville company's stoves. As a result, two things are going to happen. First, the Springfield Stove Company will go out of business. That may be unfortunate, but that happens when a company cannot match the price of a competitor. Second, by enlarging its market to include Springfield, the Pleasantville Stove Company will make more

money. It will use that money to buy newer and better machinery to make its stoves even more inexpensively. The same railroads that helped increase its stove market will also help the company bring in more iron at a quicker and cheaper rate. So the prices of the Pleasantville stoves will decrease again, perhaps to $30. At that lower price, the Pleasantville Stove Company will be able to sell stoves in more distant towns and cities. Its market will become larger. This story of two imaginary iron stove manufacturers is a perfect example of what is today called **market economy**. This essentially means that within a free economy, the price of goods is linked to supply and demand.

The development of railroads directly impacted a town's economy, including individual businesses. Lower transportation costs allowed businesses to sell their goods much farther away from where they were produced. This created greater competition between manufacturers and lower prices for consumers.

National Markets

Will the Pleasantville company keep lowering its price as its costs go down? It had better. Other stove makers are out there in other towns, ready to compete for those same markets.

Now you see how railroads made large-scale industrial production possible. Local markets like the Springfields and the Pleasantvilles of America gave way to larger markets, such as the Northeast or the Midwest. In time, these smaller regional markets led to a vast, national market in which a manufacturer in New York had to compete with manufacturers in Chicago, St. Louis, and San Francisco. Manufacturers could only compete if they became larger and more efficient. It is impossible to imagine how any of this could have happened without the railroads. Today, we live in a world where products are bought and sold from companies all over the globe. As always, the bottom line is, what is the best possible price available?

Running on Time

Did you know that it was the American railroad system that forced the introduction of time zones across the United States? Up until November 18, 1883, when four **standard time zones** were introduced, there was no standard for time. Cities and towns kept their own time based on the rising and setting of the sun in their specific locations. Because of this it wasn't possible to create accurate train timetables Gradually, large countries all over the world, inspired by America, did the same thing.

Vocabulary

"standard time zone," (phrase) an area within which everyone observes the same time

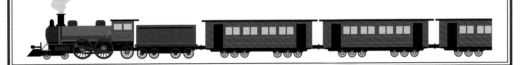

Railroads and Time Zones in 1900

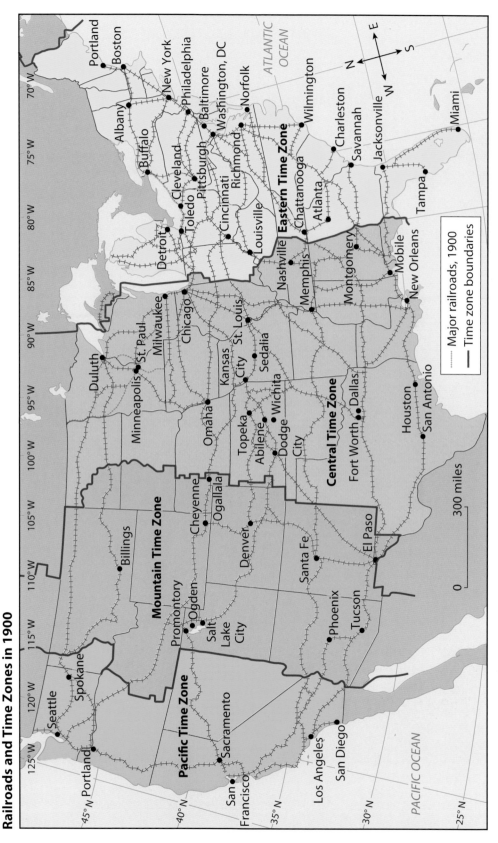

As railroads expanded across the United States, the introduction of time zones allowed accurate train schedules to be created.

Chapter 3
Resources, People, and Capital

Rich in Resources **Natural resources** contributed significantly to America's industrial growth. Few countries have had as many important natural resources as the United States. Consider coal and iron, the two main **minerals** needed by industrializing countries in the 1800s.

The Big Question

How did investment in corporations help to drive America's rapid industrial development?

Vocabulary

natural resource, n. something from nature that is useful to humans

mineral, n. a naturally occurring substance found in Earth's crust

ore, n. rock from which metal can be obtained

Even before the Civil War, Americans were mining large amounts of coal found in the ground in Pennsylvania and Ohio. Before long, additional coal fields were opened in West Virginia, Kentucky, and Illinois. By the end of the century, new mines opened in the western states of Colorado, Wyoming, and Utah. As a result, coal production rose from just three million tons in 1865 to just over two hundred million tons in 1900. As for iron, the huge amounts of this **ore** in the Mesabi Range in Minnesota made the United States the greatest producer of iron ore in the world.

Conditions inside early coal mines were dangerous. The days were long and the work was backbreaking.

Coal and iron were just two of the minerals produced by the growing United States. From the mining frontier in the West came not only gold and silver but also such important metals as copper, lead, and zinc. Meanwhile, American forests produced a seemingly endless supply of timber.

Discovering Oil

Oil was discovered in Pennsylvania in 1859. It was first used for lighting and for lubrication—the use of a substance to help machinery or equipment run more smoothly. Later in the century, it was used as fuel for motors. Even before the great discoveries of oil in Texas and California after 1900, America had more oil than it needed for its growing population.

That growing population was another factor in the nation's industrial growth. The population tripled between 1860 and 1910. Much of that increased population was made up of immigrants, people who came to the United States from other countries. They and their children made up the majority of workers in America's mines and factories. A growing population also meant a larger market for the goods those factories produced.

Children, mostly boys, were sent to work underground in coal mines. They could move through small, cramped spaces that adults could not reach.

Financial Systems

Another factor that contributed to America's growth as an industrial society was the availability of **capital**. Building a factory, buying a machine, mining ore, laying down railroad track—these projects cost a lot of money. That money generally comes from one of two sources. One is the federal, state, or local government. The other source is private savings—perhaps the savings of the people building the factory or the railroad, or the savings of others, who pay some of the costs of building the factory or railroad in exchange for a share of ownership. Or it might come from people who lend their savings to the factory or railroad builders, or from those who put their savings in a bank that then lends money to the people building the factory or railroad. As you can imagine, those investing their money expected to earn it back—and then some. In other words, they hoped the money that was invested would earn even more money.

Now consider the railroads that were built in the last thirty-five years of the 1800s. It took about $10 billion to build them. Where did all of that capital come from? Federal, state, and local governments supplied about $1 billion in gifts of land and money. That still left $9 billion for railroad companies to raise. This large amount of capital could only come from the savings of thousands of individuals. How could such savings be pooled to provide the required amount of capital?

The answer was a form of business organization known as the **corporation**. A corporation sells shares of ownership, or stock, in its business to people willing to risk some of their savings for the chance to make more money. Buyers of these shares are called stockholders. If the business does well, stockholders share in its profits. If the business does poorly, stockholders may lose some or even all of the money that they have invested.

The corporation as a form of business organization had been around since the early 1800s. However, it did not become widely used until after the Civil War. Most of the large businesses formed in the late 1800s were corporations. They attracted capital not only from American investors seeking a profit on their savings, but also from foreigners. Wealthy individuals, companies, and banks in countries such as Great Britain and France poured money into America's new industries.

Ten times as much capital was invested in American industries—from all sources—in 1900 as had been invested just thirty-five years before. Most of that was through corporations. Without the corporation, and a range of financial partnerships, America's industrial development could not have been achieved in so short a time.

Today, there are stock exchanges—centers for buying and selling partial ownership of companies—all over the world. This is a photograph of the inside of the New York Stock Exchange.

Chapter 4
An Inventive People

Finding a Better Way In Washington, D.C., there is an office called the U.S. **Patent** Office. People who think up new and useful inventions register their ideas at this office and receive a special right called a patent. That patent prohibits anyone else from using, making, or selling the invention without the inventor's permission.

The Big Question

How would you describe the inventors Alexander Graham Bell and Thomas Alva Edison?

Vocabulary

patent, n. a license from the government that gives the person requesting the patent the exclusive right to make, use, or sell an invention

Knowing the number of inventions recorded at the Patent Office gives us a pretty good idea of the inventiveness in America. In the early years of our history, the Patent Office was hardly a busy place. During the 1790s, an average of just twenty-seven inventions were recorded a year. The story was very different one century later. The Patent Office then was recording an average of 23,500 patents a year. This great burst of inventions not only tells us how successful Americans were in finding new or better ways to do things, it also helps explain the speedy growth of industrialism in America.

Most of the inventions during this time actually made only minor improvements to existing machines—a better valve here, or new gear there. But some inventions, such as the telephone, created entirely new industries and greatly increased output in others.

This is what the first commercially available telephone looked like.

Alexander Graham Bell

Alexander Graham Bell was born in Scotland in 1847. During his early years, Alexander worked alongside his father, who had dedicated his life to improving methods of communication for the deaf. In 1870, when Alexander was twenty-three years old, his father moved the

Although it does not look much like the ones we use today, this image shows Alexander speaking into a telephone receiver in 1876.

entire family to Canada. One year later, Alexander moved to Boston and began to work on the idea of transmitting the human voice over wires. Working with him was a man named Thomas Augustus Watson. Thomas worked in an electrical shop in Boston. The two men worked night and day on their invention. Finally, on March 7, 1876, Bell received a patent on his new device—the telephone. A few days later, Alexander and Thomas demonstrated that the new device actually worked. With Alexander in one room and Thomas in another, Alexander spoke these words into his device, "Mr. Watson, come here—I want to see you!" and Thomas heard him.

Fifteen years after the invention of the telephone, new factories had made a half million telephones, copper mines had produced tons of copper for telephone wires, and the lumber industry had cut thousands of trees to make the poles on which these wires were strung.

In the same way, the invention of the refrigerated railroad car, which kept beef and pork fresh while being shipped long distances, made the meatpacking industry possible. The invention of the typewriter not only created another new industry but also changed office work forever. The invention of the internal **combustion engine** made the automobile industry possible. The list could go on and on.

An Inventing Genius

Thomas Alva Edison was a man whose inventions changed the way Americans lived and also created entirely new industries.

Thomas Edison was born in Ohio in 1847. He was the youngest of seven children. Thomas had a special genius for inventing things. As a young boy he was endlessly curious. Because of childhood illnesses he did not start school until he was eight years old, and then he did not remain there long. Thomas's mother, a former schoolteacher, decided to educate Thomas at

home. However, Thomas would later say, that for the most part, he educated himself. He became interested in science, especially chemistry, the science that deals with the makeup of physical materials. At age ten he set up his own chemistry laboratory in the basement of his parents' home.

Even when Thomas, at the age of twelve, got a job selling newspapers and candy on a train, his mind remained on science. There was a lot of free time on this job, and Edison persuaded the train conductor to let him set up a chemistry laboratory in the

As a youth, Thomas Edison earned money selling candy and newspapers.

baggage car. That little project came to an end when he spilled a bottle of chemicals and set fire to the wooden floor of the car.

When he was fifteen years old, Edison (like Andrew Carnegie) learned to operate a telegraph. It was this work that turned his ever-curious mind to electricity. By the time he was nineteen, he was already thinking about making his living as an inventor.

Edison's first inventions as a full-time inventor were actually a number of improvements to the stock ticker. This machine was used in the offices of people who bought and sold shares of stocks in American companies for their customers. The stock ticker helped keep track of the prices of stocks. Edison was able to sell his inventions for $40,000, a huge sum at that time. He used the money to set up a shop in Newark, New Jersey, in 1876 to make other new inventions. He was only twenty-nine years old. Working in his small shop, Edison averaged about forty inventions a year over the course of the next five years. With one invention he figured out a way to send four messages at once over a single telegraph wire.

He then built a larger laboratory in Menlo Park, New Jersey, and hired fifteen assistants to help him with the business of inventing. This idea of an inventing team, so common today, was

Stock tickers were like telegraphs. Information about stock prices could be transmitted using them.

new at that time. Edison believed that such a team could turn out inventions as regularly as factories produced goods. He expected to turn out "a minor invention every ten days and a big one every six months or so." Amazingly, he did. In the very first year, he invented the **phonograph** and created a whole new industry.

Edison worked tirelessly. He sometimes slept only two or three hours a night. He expected his assistants to work hard, too. He once said that too many who applied for a job with him "wanted to know only two things: how much we pay and how long we work." To such people Edison growled, "Well, we don't pay anything, and we work all the time."

Here you can see Thomas Alva Edison with the **phonograph** machine that he invented.

Yet few who worked with Edison complained. One of the workers at Menlo Park explained: "Edison made your work interesting. He made me feel that I was making something with him. I wasn't just a workman." The worker then added with a smile, "And then, in those days, we all hoped to get rich with him." Some did.

Over the years, Thomas Edison invented the electric light bulb, the storage battery, the moving picture camera, and hundreds of other things that changed the way Americans lived. He also built the first central power plant to produce electricity and carry it into homes and offices.

Edison's search for a way to use electricity to light homes and offices shows how he went about making inventions. Edison first worked out a way to make a glass bulb from which all air had been pumped out. That was necessary to keep any material placed inside the bulb from burning up. (No air means no oxygen. Without oxygen, nothing can burn.) Next, he and his assistants searched for some material that would make a light when an **electric current** passed through it. The strand of material needed to be thin enough to glow but not so thin that it would crumble or melt.

Several other inventors were engaged in the same search as Edison, but it was Edison who finally succeeded. "The trouble with other inventors," he once said, "is that they try a few things and quit. I never quit until I get what I want."

After several hundred experiments, Edison's team of assistants got one material to glow for a few seconds. This was not long enough for Edison. Several hundred more experiments produced another strand of material that glowed for a minute or more. Still not long enough, said Edison. Finally, after going through sixteen hundred different materials, Edison, using a strand of thread coated with **carbon**, got a bulb to glow for more than thirteen minutes. The electric light bulb had been invented.

> ## Vocabulary
>
> **electric current,** n. the flow of electricity through a circuit
>
> **carbon,** n. a nonmetal substance that makes up diamonds and graphite and is found in coal

Here you can see an older Thomas Edison working in his laboratory.

Some years later, Edison and his assistants would spend five years conducting 10,296 experiments to improve storage batteries until Edison was satisfied with the product. That long search showed what Edison meant when he said, that genius was "one percent inspiration and ninety-nine percent perspiration."

When Edison died in 1931, some people suggested that the nation honor him by turning off all electricity for a minute or two on the day of his funeral. The idea was quickly dropped. The nation had come to depend on electricity so much that people worried that a complete cutoff, even for a minute or two, would disrupt too many things. The decision not to cut off all electricity even for a minute was the greatest tribute the nation could have paid to the genius of Thomas Edison.

Thomas Edison in His Own Words

In letters, speeches and interviews, Thomas Edison left behind a wealth of observations about his work and the nature of work in general. Here are some of the best. Maybe you have heard a few of them before.

- "I am more of a sponge than an inventor. I absorb ideas from every source."

- "I always invent to obtain money to go on inventing."

- "All you need to be an inventor is a good imagination and a pile of junk."

- "Good fortune is what happens when opportunity meets with preparation."

- "I have more respect for the fellow with a single idea who gets there than for the fellow with a thousand ideas who does nothing."

- "Your idea has to be original only in its adaptation to the problem you're working on."

- "A good idea never was lost. Its possessor may die, but it will be reborn in the mind of another."

- "If we all did the things we are capable of doing, we would literally astound ourselves."

- "Restlessness is discontent and discontent is the first necessity of progress. Show me a thoroughly satisfied man and I will show you a failure."

- "Everything comes to him who hustles while he waits."

- "If I find 10,000 ways something won't work, I haven't failed. I am not discouraged, because every wrong attempt discarded is another step forward. Just because something doesn't do what you planned it to do doesn't mean it's useless."

- "The three things that are essential to achievement are hard work, stick-to-it-iv-ness, and common sense."

- "Opportunity is missed by most people because it is dressed in overalls and looks like work."

- "There seems to be no limit to which some men will go to avoid the labor of thinking. Thinking is hard work."

- "None of my inventions came about totally by accident; they came by hard work. Genius is one percent inspiration and ninety-nine percent perspiration."

- "The thing I lose patience with the most is the clock. Its hands move too fast. Time is really the only capital that any human being has, and the one thing that he can't afford to lose."

- "From his neck down a man is worth a couple of dollars a day, from his neck up he is worth anything that his brain can produce."

- "I have always found, when I was worrying, that the best thing to do was put my mind upon something, work hard and forget what was troubling me."

- "I never perfected an invention that I did not think about in terms of the service it might give others."

- "Of all my inventions I liked the phonograph best."

- "I am proud of the fact that I never invented weapons to kill."

Thomas Edison never stopped working and coming up with new ideas. He may very well be one of the greatest inventors of all time.

Chapter 5
Growing Business Enterprises

Leaders of Business There were several reasons the United States grew into a strong industrial society. Railroads, natural resources, a growing population, available capital, and new inventions all played a part. It also took the vision, courage, and creativity of a group of American business leaders to ensure success.

The Big Question

Why do you think Andrew Carnegie and John D. Rockefeller were so successful?

This is a steam train from the 1930s leaving a railway station in Chicago. Improved methods of transportation were one of the reasons why America became such a strong industrial nation.

Coming from many different backgrounds, these business leaders were men of imagination and **enterprise**. They were bold and adventurous individuals willing to take risks and oversee large projects. Often, they were among the first to see how an invention or a new process could be turned into a profitable business. Most of them had a genius for organization. All of them had a driving ambition for wealth and power.

Andrew Carnegie and Steel

One of the most enterprising was Andrew Carnegie, the young Scottish immigrant who started out as a bobbin boy. You will recall that Carnegie went to work for railroad man Tom Scott at age seventeen, invested his pay wisely, and had a sizable income by his early thirties. Carnegie could easily have retired from work right then and lived well for the rest of his life. But retirement did not fit in with this ambitious young man's plans. He knew that America was just entering a period of great economic growth. He was determined to be a part of it.

In 1865, Carnegie bought a company that made iron bridges. Years later, he explained this move: "With all the new railroad construction," he said, "I saw it would never do to depend further upon wooden bridges for permanent railway structures." Hiring the best iron makers and bridge designers he could find, Carnegie turned his company into the country's leading maker of iron bridges.

Soon after, Carnegie shifted his focus to making steel. The advantages of steel over iron had been known for hundreds of years. Steel is stronger, easier to work with, and less likely to break. The problem was that to make steel, you had to burn out **impurities** from melted iron. At the time, no one knew how to do that quickly and cheaply. It took several weeks of heating, stirring, and reheating iron to make just fifty pounds of steel.

The Eads Bridge was the first all-steel bridge construction. It was financed by Andrew Carnegie and opened in 1874. In its day, it was the longest arch bridge in the world. The bridge goes over the Mississippi River and connects St. Louis, Missouri, and East St. Louis, Illinois. In the photographs you can see the bridge being constructed in 1870 (top) and the bridge today.

In the 1850s, an American named William Kelly and an Englishman named Henry Bessemer, working independently, each discovered how to burn the impurities out of iron quickly and cheaply by forcing a stream of air into melted iron. By the 1870s, Bessemer "open furnaces" in England were turning thirty thousand pounds of iron into steel in a matter of minutes.

One visit to a Bessemer furnace in England in 1872 convinced Andrew Carnegie that steel was the metal of the future. By the early 1880s, railroads had reached the huge underground stores of iron ore discovered in Michigan and Minnesota. It was now possible to bring this ore by railroad to a port on the Great Lakes, then by ship across the lakes (usually to Cleveland), and finally by railroad again to Pittsburgh, Pennsylvania. Pittsburgh—with its closeness to coal mines, three good rivers, and rail transportation—became the center of the steel industry. Carnegie promptly sold his iron bridge company and built a large plant for making steel near Pittsburgh.

Carnegie's new steel mill prospered. Carnegie had many acquaintances in the railroad industry, going back to his days with Tom Scott. He had little trouble convincing them of the advantages of his steel rails—the rail being the main

the rail

At the Bessemer furnace in England, Andrew Carnegie saw how workers were able to burn the impurities out of iron in order to quickly make steel.

Andrew Carnegie convinced many railroad owners to switch to steel rails.

part of the railway track—over the iron ones they had been using. Among other things, steel rails lasted twenty times longer than iron rails. Orders poured in. As his business grew, Carnegie hired the ablest people he could find to help him run it. He insisted on efficiency and on controlling costs. "Watch the costs," he was fond of saying, "and the profits will take care of themselves."

Carnegie put his profits right back into his company. He bought the latest equipment. He invested in mines that produced iron, coal, and limestone, which are the basic ingredients for making steel. He bought boats and railroads to bring those ingredients and everything else that he needed to his steel mills. As a result, Carnegie could make steel more cheaply than anyone else.

Cutting the Competition

In 1880, there were about one thousand other companies that made iron and steel. Most, however, were unable to compete with the quality and price of Carnegie's steel. Carnegie bought a number of the more **efficient** companies, allowing him to increase his lead over the others that remained.

Andrew Carnegie had a remarkable ability to see changes coming and to adjust to them before others did. You already saw how he left the iron bridge business and jumped into steel ahead of the crowd. He did the same in the 1880s, when he was making a fortune by manufacturing steel rails for the railroad industry. Carnegie saw that as cities grew, there would be a demand for steel for constructing tall buildings. Even as orders for railroad tracks poured in, he began to shift production to steel beams for buildings. When the demand for this steel became strong, Carnegie was ready.

> **Vocabulary**
>
> **efficient,** adj.
> productive without wasting time or resources

What were the results of Andrew Carnegie's business genius? One was that by the 1890s, Carnegie's steel plants produced nearly as much steel as all his American rivals put together. Another was that Andrew Carnegie became an a very rich man, possibly the second richest man in the world at that time.

Here you can see the Carnegie Steel Company in Pittsburgh, Pennsylvania.

Most important, due to Carnegie's accomplishments, the United States became the largest maker of steel in the world, and its people moved quickly toward becoming an industrial society.

John D. Rockefeller and Oil

The story of the oil industry, like the story of steel, starts in western Pennsylvania, but it is quite different. People had long been aware of the oil that seeped through rock and floated on the creeks of that region. However, they regarded this oil as a nuisance, for they believed it had no real uses. In the 1850s, however, a chemistry professor at Yale University developed a simple method for refining—that is, removing the impurities from—this "Pennsylvania rock oil" so it could be used to make kerosene, a liquid fuel also known as paraffin, for lighting lamps. After 1900, oil became valuable as a fuel for automobiles and other machinery. If anyone now could find a way to get this oil out of the ground in large enough amounts, it would be quite valuable.

The first commercially successful oil well was drilled at Titusville, Pennsylvania, in 1859. Many potential oil men quickly flocked to the region to drill for the "black gold," as oil was called. It was like the California Gold Rush all over again. The drillers shipped their **crude oil** to nearby Cleveland, Ohio, where a few men had started oil **refineries**.

The first American oil well, seen here, was in Titusville, Pennsylvania.

In Cleveland, a young man named John D. Rockefeller followed developments in Pennsylvania with great interest. Rockefeller was a serious, religious man with an eye for detail and a head for business. He had already made money in a wholesale grocery business. Now, at age twenty-seven, he decided to give oil a try.

As the nearest large city to the Pennsylvania oil fields, Cleveland already had some thirty small companies to which the oil was shipped for refining. In 1867, Rockefeller bought one of these refineries.

Why did Rockefeller buy a refinery, and not some oil wells? The reason was that while there was fierce competition in every part of the oil business, it was most fierce in the

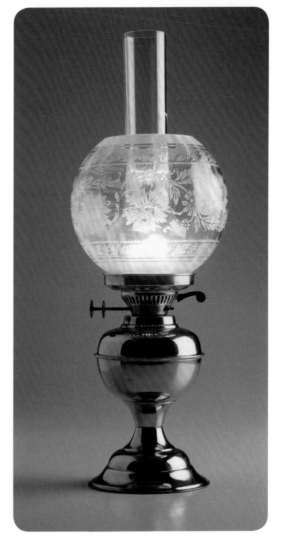

Before electricity, kerosene, a byproduct of oil, was an important source of fuel for lamps and stoves.

oil fields. Hundreds and even thousands of drillers, hoping to get rich quick, were producing far more oil than refiners were ready to buy. That pushed down the prices the drillers received. Rockefeller did not like this kind of confusion in business.

Here is where Rockefeller showed his special genius. Rockefeller saw that the key to the oil business was the refining part. If he could gain control of refining, he could dominate the entire oil industry. If he could become the only buyer of crude oil, he could decide what price to offer the drillers. They would have to take it or leave it. As the only seller of refined oil, he could set the price customers would have to pay for it.

In 1870, Rockefeller made his first move to control the oil industry. He formed a corporation called the Standard Oil Company. Then he offered to buy all the other Cleveland refineries. To those who agreed to sell, Rockefeller paid a generous price. To those who refused, he became a ruthless enemy.

John D. Rockefeller as a young man

Kerosene was an important product refined from oil. Kerosene was burned in lamps and stoves to provide light and heat. Rockefeller cut the price of kerosene so far that his competitors lost money on every sale. So did Standard Oil, of course, but Rockefeller knew he could outlast the others. Once his competitors had been driven out of business, he could raise prices and make money again. Within two years, Standard Oil controlled nearly every refinery in Cleveland. Success led to more success. A few years later Rockefeller bought refineries in New York, Philadelphia, Baltimore, and Pittsburgh as well.

Rockefeller was a smart and ruthless businessman who returned his immense profits back into his business to make it bigger and more efficient. Soon, Standard Oil was manufacturing its own chemicals for refining, building its own warehouses for storing, making its own barrels for shipping, and making its own cans for selling the oil to consumers.

Like Carnegie, Rockefeller paid attention to every small detail to keep down his costs. One day, Rockefeller was inspecting one of his factories that filled and sealed five-gallon tin cans of kerosene. He watched as a machine attached the tops to the cans with small drops of solder (/sah*der/), a liquid metal that hardens quickly.

"How many drops of solder do you use on each can?" Rockefeller asked the man in charge.

"Forty," replied the man.

"Have you ever tried thirty eight?" asked Rockefeller. "No? Would you mind having some [cans] sealed with thirty-eight and let me know?"

The worker did as Rockefeller requested. Thirty-eight drops, it turned out, sealed most cans tightly, but a few leaked. But thirty-nine created a perfect seal each time! That difference of one drop, from forty to thirty-nine, saved Standard Oil $2,500 the first year. Over the years, the savings grew to hundreds of thousands of dollars.

Up to that point, Rockefeller had succeeded mainly by being more efficient than his competitors. Before long, however, Rockefeller's Standard Oil Company was using more questionable business tactics to beat its rivals. These tactics raised serious concerns over how the new industrial giants, or robber barons as they became known, were using their power.

J.P. Morgan

Another extraordinarily powerful and influential person from this era was J.P. Morgan (1837–1913). J.P. Morgan was a wealthy banker who invested in railroad companies. J.P. Morgan was involved with Thomas Edison's company when it became part of General Electric. J.P. Morgan financed steel companies, and is thought to have been one of the richest men in American history. J.P. Morgan had a particular love of art, and much of what he collected is on display at the Morgan Library and Museum in New York.

Some of J.P. Morgan's book collection can be see here.

Chapter 6
Monopolies, Trusts, and Pools

Corporate Bully By the 1870s, Standard Oil had become a giant in the oil industry. Like many giants, it could throw its weight around to gain advantage over its rivals—and it did.

The Big Question

What were the perceived advantages and disadvantages of large and powerful businesses?

Vocabulary

freight, n. shipped goods; cargo

One thing Rockefeller did was to play railroad companies against one another. Rockefeller told each railroad that if it wanted his business, it would have to give Standard Oil a rebate, or discount. That is, it would have to pay Standard back a portion of its **freight** charges. And it must do this secretly. Desperate for Standard Oil's business, each of the railroads agreed. So while his competitors in Ohio were paying thirty-five cents to transport a barrel of oil, Rockefeller was paying only ten cents.

As Standard Oil became larger and more powerful, Rockefeller's demands grew even bolder. To keep Standard Oil's business, a railroad now had to pay a rebate on everything Standard Oil shipped. It also had to give Standard Oil a rebate on everything its competitors shipped. The railroads gave in.

As a result, Rockefeller was able to get a stranglehold on the oil-refining industry. By 1879, Rockefeller controlled 90 percent of the refining business in the country.

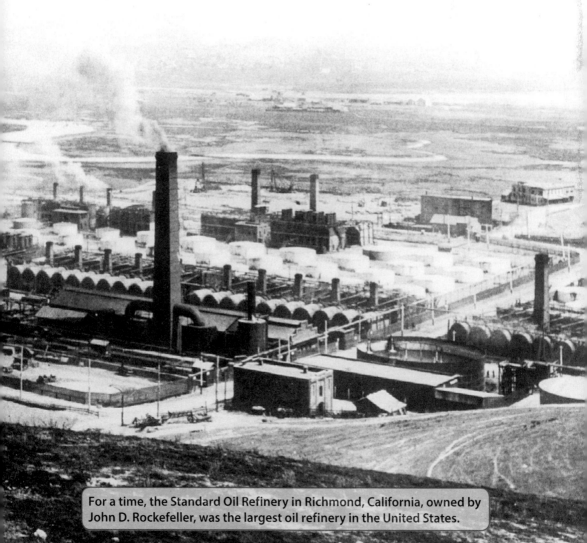

For a time, the Standard Oil Refinery in Richmond, California, owned by John D. Rockefeller, was the largest oil refinery in the United States.

That was practically a **monopoly**, the complete control of an industry by a single company.

To tighten its grip further, in 1882 Standard Oil adopted a new form of organization called a **trust**. Here is how a trust worked: Stockholders of different companies in the same industry—in this case, oil—turned over their stocks to a single group of **trustees**. In return, the stockholders received trust certificates. Trust certificates entitled them to share in the profits of the trust. But the stockholders also gave up any say in how each of their own companies would be run. That was left to the trustees.

Using the trust form of organization, Standard Oil brought thirty-nine more oil companies under its control. By then, it controlled almost the entire oil business.

The trust idea caught on quickly. Soon there was a tobacco trust, a leather trust, a sugar trust, and a dozen others. By 1900, in fact, two-thirds of all manufactured goods in the United States were produced by just a handful of giant corporations like these trusts.

Trusts and American Consumers

In the latter years of the 1800s, more Americans became concerned about the size of some businesses. Most recognized that large businesses could produce goods at a lower cost than small companies could. That meant they could sell their goods to the American consumer for less.

But did they?

Sometimes, yes; sometimes, no. Even while making large profits, Standard Oil passed on its lower costs to its customers. So did Andrew Carnegie's steel companies and a few others. However, most companies did not. In fact, one of the main reasons for forming a trust was to control production and keep prices up without fear of competition.

Americans were concerned about what the trusts were doing to open opportunity in business. The chance to go into any business a person wanted was an old idea and tradition in the United States. Some who entered business would succeed, while others would fail. But trusts and huge businesses, it was feared, had the power to put an end to opportunity altogether. They could force small companies out of business and squash anyone who wanted to enter their field.

People also feared big business's growing influence in local, state, and even national politics. Not only could their money help elect representatives friendly to them, it could also bribe officials to make decisions that benefited the companies.

New Millionaires

Furthermore, the creation of great industries, such as steel and oil, had led to the growth of huge fortunes. Before the Civil War, there were only a handful of millionaires in America. By 1900, there were more than four thousand. A few of these owned so much wealth that ordinary people could hardly grasp the meaning of the numbers. Andrew Carnegie's total fortune was more than half a billion dollars, the equivalent of around $9 or $10 billion today.

John D. Rockefeller was a billionaire. Railroad giants Cornelius Vanderbilt and his son William were not far behind. James B. Duke had made hundreds of millions of dollars from the tobacco industry. Gustavus Swift and Philip Armour made their fortunes in the meatpacking industry.

This period in American history of great industrial and financial growth became known as the Gilded Age. It was a name given to it by the author Mark Twain because many people felt that although things looked good on the surface—big businesses, growing wealth, and for some a glitzy lifestyle, underneath there was corruption and also suffering. To many Americans,

This cartoon by George Luks shows a growing distrust of the big businesses, or trusts, and the power and influence they could have over people's lives.

the growing gap between these few wealthy men and millions of middle class Americans—and the even larger gap between the wealthy and the poor—was a problem. Americans might applaud the ambition and talent that helped Andrew Carnegie become wealthy, but they worried that for every Andrew Carnegie that industrialism had produced, there were thousands of poor, out-of-work people like Tom O'Donnell, the struggling worker you read about in Chapter 1.

Not all people shared this worry, though. Some regarded these fortunes as the just rewards of hard work and enterprise. These "captains of industry" had led America into the Industrial Age. Some people felt the whole society benefited from their efforts. Furthermore, the fact that at least some had started out as poor boys seemed to prove that opportunity was still open to any person of ability.

In addition to providing inspiration to others, some of the men of great wealth gave generously to charities to improve life in America. Moved by the

John D. Rockefeller donated millions of dollars to build the University of Chicago.

spirit of "earn and give," they spent part of their fortunes to build museums, parks, hospitals, universities, and concert halls to be enjoyed by all. John D. Rockefeller gave millions to create the University of Chicago and to finance medical research. Andrew Carnegie provided money to build free public libraries in hundreds of America's towns and cities.

Still, Americans debated whether the leaders of big business were true "captains of industry" who generously helped society, or were "robber barons" who made money by taking advantage of society and contributing little in return.

Controlling Big Business

As a result, many Americans began to look to the government to **regulate** large and powerful businesses. They wanted government to control how large corporations did business. By far, the single largest industry in the United States at the time was the railroad industry. So it was railroads that the U.S. government first attempted to regulate.

> **Vocabulary**
>
> **regulate,** v. to control or place limits on

There were three main unfair practices that railroad companies engaged in. One was the practice of giving rebates to favored shippers, which you have already read about.

A second unfair practice was called "pooling." From time to time, railroad companies using the same routes agreed to stop competing with one another. They worked out a formula whereby each company controlled traffic on a certain portion of the route. Thus, company A would carry 35 percent of the traffic; company B, 28 percent; company C, 23 percent; and so on.

That was the pool. Each then pledged to take no more than its assigned share and to charge exactly the same high price for carrying freight on that route. As long as the companies stuck to their agreement (which they often did not), customers would have to pay whatever the railroads demanded.

The third unfair practice was common on routes where there was only a single railroad. Without competition, a railroad could charge unreasonably high rates. For example, compare the rates east of Chicago, where there was competition, with rates west of the Missouri River, where there was none. East of Chicago, railroads charged ninety-five cents a mile for a ton of freight (when there was no pool). West of the Missouri River the charge was $4.80—more than five times as much.

Who was hurt by these unfair business practices of the railroads? Every business shipping goods had to pay more to get its goods to customers. But to stay in business, these companies raised their prices and passed their costs on to their customers. So all across America, people paid more for food and manufactured goods. People like Tom O'Donnell had to pay more for a loaf of bread or a pair of shoes for his children, if he could afford the bread and shoes in the first place.

Freight trains carried goods all across the country.

The difference went into the pockets of the already wealthy owners of the railroads and their shareholders.

New Laws

In 1887, the U.S. Congress attempted to deal with these problems by passing the Interstate **Commerce** Act. This law outlawed both railroad pools and rebates. The law also made it illegal to charge more for carrying goods short distances than for long ones along the same route. To see that the law was carried out, Congress also created the Interstate Commerce Commission. However, Congress did not give this new commission enough power to do its job well. Even when the commission did try to act, the courts often overturned its rulings.

Attempts to stop the growth of trusts and monopolies were no more effective. In 1890, Congress passed the Sherman Antitrust Act. This law declared that trusts and other forms of business intended to restrict trade were illegal. However, the wording of the Sherman Antitrust Act was vague, and corporations soon found ways to get around the new law. Money talked and **free enterprise** ruled. The wealthy business owners worked hard to keep government out of their affairs. Even when the government did occasionally charge a business with wrongdoing, the courts usually sided with the business. Big business was so powerful that it was able to influence how judges interpreted the law. The number of trusts and monopolies continued to grow.

> **Vocabulary**
>
> **commerce,** n. the buying and selling of goods and services; trade
>
> **free enterprise,** n. a system in which businesses operate with minimal government involvement

Chapter 7
The World of the Worker

From Farm to Factory So far you have read about the leaders of industrialism. Men like Andrew Carnegie and John D. Rockefeller were famous for their skill in business, their great wealth, and their generosity.

The Big Question

What were some of the advantages and disadvantages for American workers during this period of change?

But industrialism was not about just a few fabulously wealthy people. It was also about millions of working people like Tom O'Donnell whose lives were changed, not always for the better, by the growth of industry in America.

Before the arrival of industrialism, the vast majority of Americans were farmers. Most made whatever goods they needed for daily living—clothing, shoes, furniture, candles—for themselves in their spare time. These goods were not fancy, but they worked.

At this time, there were also goods for sale made by skilled workers who were known as craftsmen. People with money could buy shoes, clothing, tools, and other goods. A craftsman made his entire product from beginning to end. A shoemaker, for example, cut the leather, hammered it, shaped it, and stitched it. Craftsmen were respected in their communities for their skills. Often they worked for themselves in their own homes or small shops, and they set their own hours. When they worked for someone else, their employer was usually a craftsman, too, who worked right alongside them. That employer knew not only

Before the Industrial Age, a shoemaker might work at home, teaching his skill to a son, or he might work in a small shop where he could sell the shoes he made.

his workers but also their families. He joined in their celebrations and shared in their sorrows.

All this changed as large factories replaced small workshops. To begin with, no longer did one worker make a product from beginning to end. The work of making each product was broken down into many separate steps—shoemaking alone had sixty-four separate steps. Each worker was assigned to do the same task over and over, day after day. In shoemaking, one worker would spend the day cutting leather, while another stitched shoes, and a third nailed heels into place.

Even without machines, dividing up the work this way, with each worker specializing in a single step, allowed the same number of workers to produce more shoes. The work was less varied, and less skill was needed.

The Machine Age

In time, machines took over much of the work, and this affected craftsmen. In earlier days, it took years for a skilled worker to learn how to make shoes or cloth well. But now, complained a craftsman with thirty years of experience, "You can take a boy fresh from the farm, and in three days he can manage a machine as well as I can." So could a young woman from the nearby countryside. So could a newly arrived, unskilled immigrant. The employer paid all of them much less than a skilled worker would otherwise earn.

How could a skilled worker compete with that? The answer, of course, is that he could not. Many had to give up their trades. Some became factory workers themselves.

Unlike the craftsman of old who employed four or five workers, factories hired hundreds or even thousands. It was rare that an owner knew his workers by name, and rarer still that he knew much about their lives. Workers became just another cost of production. In the competition among businesses, each owner sought to keep those costs down. If that meant cutting wages or letting some workers go, then so be it. Tom

As a result of mass production, the prices of individual items fell.

O'Donnell, you may recall, had only fifteen weeks of work the year he appeared before the U.S. Senate committee.

Factory workers usually worked ten to twelve hours a day, six days a week. More hours of daylight during the summer months meant that many worked thirteen- or fourteen-hour days. Actually, long workdays were not that unusual in the 1800s. Farmers, for example, had always worked long hours. So had many skilled workers, working in their homes and shops. What was different about working in industrial society were the working conditions.

Factories ran strictly by the clock. "The rule was that the men had to be in the [factory] before the whistle blew [at 6:00 a.m.]," explained one worker.

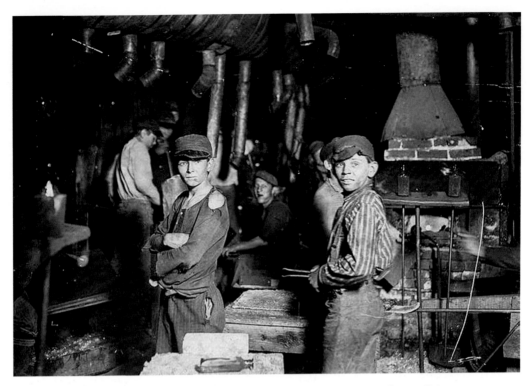
Men, women, and children worked long hours, often in harsh, unsafe conditions.

"If a man was half or even quarter of a minute late he was shut out . . . until nine o'clock, so that he would make only three-quarters of a day's work."

Working conditions were often dangerous as well as difficult. These were the days before the widespread use of electricity. Buildings were dimly lit and had little fresh air. Workers were not protected from dangerous machinery. A single slip, a moment of inattention, could cost a life or a limb.

For the several million people who worked on railroads, in mines, and in lumbering, work was especially dangerous. On railroads alone, more than seven thousand workers were killed and another thirty-three thousand injured in a typical year like 1891. Thousands of miners died young as a result of coal dust in their lungs. Others died when their mines caved in on them. Not a year went by without at least a thousand miners being killed and fifty thousand injured.

By 1900, the United States had one of the highest industrial accident rates among industrialized countries. Each year, more than twenty thousand workers were killed and two hundred thousand were injured. For the families of those killed, there was no assistance except what fellow workers might contribute. Nor was there any pay for injured workers while they were off the job and no help with their doctors' bills. Often, when injured workers were ready to return to work, they found their jobs filled by others.

Women, too, suffered from these long hours and unhealthy conditions. Near the end of the 1800s, 20 percent of workers in manufacturing were women. In the **garment** industry—the industry that made dresses and clothing—women made up the majority of workers. These women worked side by side at their sewing machines in hot, airless rooms, rooms so uncomfortable they came to be called **sweatshops**. They did the same work as men, but they received only half the pay.

The garment industry employed more women than men.

Many workers in the new industrial society were children. Indeed, American factories had a long history of child labor. More than half the workers in Samuel Slater's very first cotton mill were children under the age of ten. By the 1890s, nearly one hundred thousand children worked in America's factories and mines.

The coal mining industry employed thousands of young boys. Some worked underground, driving the mules that hauled the coal-filled carts out of the mines. During most of the year, these boys saw daylight only on Sundays.

Most of the boys at the mines, though, worked on the surface as "breaker boys." Coal came out of the mine in large chunks. These chunks were then crushed into smaller lumps by heavy rollers, or breakers. The breaker boy's job was to separate out the pieces of slate that remained among the lumps of coal. Here is how one observer described the work—and remember, the breaker boy he is writing about is just about your age:

> The boy must sit on his bench all day, bending over constantly to look down on the coal that is passing beneath him. His tender hands become toughened by long and constant contact with sharp pieces of slate and coal.

Breaker boys were very young boys who worked long hours six days a week separating coal from slate. It was backbreaking work. These breaker boys were employed in a coal mine in Pittston, Pennsylvania.

Many cuts and bruises have left marks and scars on them for a lifetime. He must breathe an atmosphere thick with the dust of coal, so thick that one can barely see across the room. . . . It is no wonder that . . . his lungs are liable to suffer from the disease known as miner's **consumption**.

Vocabulary
....

consumption, n. a disease that causes the body to waste away, generally over a long period of time; tuberculosis

In cotton mills in the South, it was not unusual for boys and girls under ten years old to work up to twelve hours a day or to work at night. Supervisors kept child workers on the night shift from falling asleep by throwing cold water on them from time to time.

Of course, children who worked did not go to school. So they had little opportunity to improve themselves and escape from poverty. Their childhood was one without play. Many people were aware of this injustice to children. One poet wrote of the unfairness of child labor in these bitter lines:

> The golf links [golf course] lie so near the mill
> That almost every day
> The laboring children can look out
> And see the men at play.

The poem makes the point that rich men had the time to play, but poor children did not. This state of affairs may seem incredible to us today. But one hundred years ago, it was largely taken for granted.

Yet not all the changes that industrialization brought to the lives of working people were harmful. Indeed, the new age of factories and giant corporations brought many benefits. New inventions enriched the lives of many Americans and made life easier. Industrialism made it possible to buy a broad variety of goods at lower prices. Thanks to the cost-saving methods that steelmakers like Andrew Carnegie introduced, the price of steel fell from $160 a ton in 1875 to just $17 a ton in 1900.

Ordinary consumers did not buy steel rails and beams, of course. But they did buy pans, nails, wire, and many other products made of steel. The lower price of steel meant that these goods, too, could be made and sold at lower prices. At the same time, a ready-made clothing industry made it possible for working people to buy suits, shirts, dresses, coats, and other items they could not have afforded fifty years earlier. In addition, the new canned food and meatpacking industries changed the diets of millions of Americans.

Also, even as machines replaced thousands of weavers, shoemakers, and other craftsmen, the machines themselves were creating a demand for new skills. **Engineers** were needed to design machines, and skilled **machinists** were needed to operate them, or to build and repair them. No large factory could run without people skilled in managing its operations. Nor could a manufacturer stay in business long without traveling salespeople to find buyers for their goods. As banks and insurance companies grew, they too needed people with skills in **accounting**, bookkeeping, and managing.

And inventions like the typewriter and the telephone created thousands of jobs for women as secretaries and telephone operators. Big corporations required thousands of office workers to keep their businesses running smoothly.

Many of the workers with new skills earned good wages. Skilled workers were able to advance in their companies and become managers. These workers were able to improve their living conditions, and their children could hope for a better life than that of their parents. For skilled workers, industrialism was welcomed. It greatly expanded the size of the American middle class and created many opportunities for upward mobility. This helped fuel the view that all things were possible and America was indeed the land of opportunity.

For unskilled workers, however, industrialism was often a very different story. Some unskilled workers managed to learn new skills and improve their fortunes. Yet for millions of unskilled workers like Tom O'Donnell, the factory age brought hardships. The new world of industrialism seemed to promise those workers little more than low wages, uncertain employment, and an uncertain future for their children.

Photo: Cassell
& Co., Ltd.

A LADY TYPIST AT WORK.

The invention of the typewriter revolutionized office work and gave many young women a chance to work outside the home.

Chapter 8
Workers Organize

Banding Together Industrialism improved the lives of many Americans, especially the owners of big businesses who made great fortunes. Many other Americans—business and shop owners—found that industrialism brought them more money and more **conveniences** than they had before.

The Big Question

What is a union, and what did Samuel Gompers do to change how unions were organized?

Some workers also benefited, although generally a good deal less than the owners. The question facing workers in America's mines and new factories was, how could they improve their working conditions and their pay?

Vocabulary

convenience, n. something that makes life easier or more comfortable

Workers could not hope to change their conditions by acting alone. No individual worker, especially one who was unskilled and easily replaceable, could hope to bargain for better wages or hours with an employer. Even skilled workers had very little power or control over their wages and working conditions.

This image shows women protesting during a miners' strike. Sometimes mine owners, and even factory owners, found other workers to replace those on strike.

Trade Unions

Some workers, however, began to see that they might increase their chances of improving wages and working conditions if they banded together to form a **union**.

Union members elected leaders to bargain with employers on their behalf. If the employer refused to make the improvements workers asked for, union members would sometimes go on strike, or stop working until an agreement was reached. Workers did not earn any pay during a strike. However, if enough workers stopped working, the owner quite often had to close the business during the strike and did not make money, either.

Unions were not new to America in the late 1800s. They had been around since the 1820s and 1830s. But those early unions were mostly weak and unsuccessful, and most of them died out before the Civil War. Organizing a labor union in the late 1800s was not easy, especially among unskilled workers. Keeping it going was even harder. Owners strongly opposed unions. It was usually in their interest to keep wages low. And then there was the political threat of large groups of workers banding together. All of this sounded too much like **socialism** for some. One mine owner said, "I . . . will employ no one that belongs to any labor organization, and will at once discharge [fire] . . . any man who has anything to do with any labor organization."

When workers did manage to form a union, employers often refused to talk with their leaders.

Workers who went on strike risked losing their jobs, because employers might hire others to take their place. Some companies even hired private armies to do battle with strikers. During the early days of the labor movement, there was a great deal of violence on both sides.

Even so, some strikes in the late 1880s were successful, and in these instances, the striking unions got at least part of what they wanted. When that happened, more workers became union members. More often, however, striking unions found themselves on the losing side of the battle.

Very often, workers, running out of both money and hope, went back to work without gaining anything. Many dropped out of their unions, and others decided not to join. As a result, unions grew very slowly in the late 1800s.

The labor movement suffered a crippling blow in 1886 as a result of an incident that actually had little to do with the labor union movement. During a strike for an eight-hour workday at the McCormick Harvester Company in Chicago, workers clashed with police. One worker was killed and several others were injured. A group of **anarchists** called a protest rally at Haymarket Square the next day. The rally was orderly. As police moved in near the end, someone—no one knows who—threw a bomb, killing seven people. Eight anarchists were tried and convicted. Four were executed.

> ## Vocabulary
>
> **anarchist,** n.
> a person who rebels against or works to disrupt an established authority, usually a government or an economic system

Labor unions had little to do with the rally at Haymarket Square. However, in the minds of many Americans, labor unions became connected with the violence there. Public opinion turned against unions, and many members dropped out.

The strongest unions were those made up of skilled workers organized along the lines of their special trades, or skills. There was a union for carpenters, another for brewers, and another for cigar makers. Such unions brought together workers who shared the same problems, agreed on common goals, and would stick together to reach them. That gave them more bargaining power with their employers and, if they did go on strike, a better chance of winning. Employers knew they could not replace their striking skilled workers as easily as they could their unskilled workers.

A mass meeting called by anarchists in Chicago's Haymarket Square on May 4, 1886, turned into a riot.

Samuel Gompers and the American Federation of Labor

A member of the cigar makers' union became the most important figure in the American labor movement of his time. Samuel Gompers was born in England in 1850, the son of Dutch immigrants. The Gompers family was poor, and Samuel had to drop out of school after only a few years to help earn money for his family. By the time he was ten, he was a full-time worker learning his father's trade, cigar making.

Hoping to escape a life of poverty in England, the Gompers family moved to the United States in 1863. As it turned out, they simply exchanged their London slum for one in New York. A slaughterhouse stood on the New York street opposite theirs. A brewery stood on the street behind. In their home, from early morning until night, father and son rolled tobacco leaves into cigars.

After a year, Samuel got a job in one of New York City's cigar-making shops. That was when his education about employers and unions began. When the

Just like the boy in the photograph, Samuel Gompers made cigars when he was young.

cigar makers in his shop decided to form a union, Samuel, now fourteen, joined. Unable to win improvements from their employer, the union went on strike.

The strike was unsuccessful. The employer fired Gompers and all the others who had participated. Not only that, the employer also sent the names of the strikers to other cigar factories in the city, warning against hiring these troublemakers. Such a list of names is known as a **blacklist**.

Unable to find work at his trade in New York, Gompers took whatever jobs he could get in nearby New Jersey. Only after a year and a half was he able once again to get work in a cigar-making shop in New York. The experience of losing a strike and being blacklisted was one part of Samuel Gompers's early education on unions.

A second part came in the cigar factory itself. In the cigar factories of those days, workers did their work by hand. Following a long tradition among many workers, they took turns reading aloud newspapers, magazines, and books. In a cigar shop, there was no machinery to drown out the voice of the reader. The rest of the workers chipped in to make up for the work time the reader lost. As they rolled the cigars, the workers discussed the important political and social news of the day. It was a way of both being entertained and learning while working.

Examining His Options

During these discussions, Samuel Gompers began to think seriously about the problems of labor in an industrial society. What was the best course of action for workers to take? Should workers join movements aimed at making long-term changes for all of society? If so, what should those changes be? Or should workers simply aim at protecting themselves and improving their own working conditions? Should they form their own political party to work for improvements for workers? Or should they stay out of politics and stick to forming labor unions?

Some workers spoke in favor of reforming all the ills of society by changing the system of business ownership. The government, said these people, should take over all businesses and run the economy. Only then would all workers receive a fair wage. In Europe, workers facing the same problems largely turned to socialism.

After giving the issue a lot of thought, Gompers came to the conclusion that the best course for workers was to organize unions along the lines of their trades—meaning the kind of work they did. They should forget about socialism, or trying to change society in some distant future. Instead, they should stick to winning gains for their members in the present, concentrating on "bread-and-butter" issues such as wages, hours of work, job security (not being fired), and safety in the workplace. They also should be prepared to strike to win them. Gompers later said he could sum up his beliefs about the goals of unions in six words: "more, more, more; now, now, now."

Gompers now devoted his efforts to that cause. He organized a new branch of the cigar makers' union, and at twenty-five he was elected its president. He then turned his efforts to strengthening the national cigar makers' union.

Uniting Trade Unions

In 1886, Gompers and the leaders of several other unions who represented highly skilled workers decided to bring their trade unions together and form the American Federation of Labor (AFL). The AFL was a kind of union of trade unions. It helped promote the member unions' work to gain new members and tried to settle problems that arose among them. The trade unions in the AFL helped one another by supporting one another's strikes. For example, if the hat makers' union went on strike against a company, members of the other trade unions in the AFL might then boycott, or refuse to buy, hats made by that company. Gompers was elected the first president of the AFL, and he was reelected every year except one until his death in 1924.

The AFL grew slowly at first. While several of its member unions achieved successes, some experienced severe setbacks. Perhaps the worst setback for the unions occurred in 1892. In that year, the Carnegie steel plant in Homestead, Pennsylvania, announced a wage cut. The ironworkers' union went on strike to regain its members' lost wages.

Samuel Gompers was one of the founders of the American Federation of Labor (AFL) and was one of the most important leaders of the American labor movement.

During a strike, business owners often hired replacement workers to do the jobs of the striking workers. Union members called these people strikebreakers or scabs. Union members would set up a picket line at the entrance of the factory to prevent the strikebreakers from entering. Not all strikes were violent, but in the early days of unions, violence instead of bargaining was common.

At Homestead, Carnegie's managers had no interest in bargaining with striking workers. Management's aim was to break the union so the company's owners and managers could treat workers as they pleased. When union workers set up their picket line, the managers of the steel mill brought in three hundred heavily armed men from the Pinkerton detective agency to battle the strikers. Men on both sides were killed. After several months, the strikers gave up. The company took back only 10 percent of the workers and fired and blacklisted the rest. The loss of this strike nearly destroyed the ironworkers' union, as its membership fell by two-thirds.

Such setbacks kept American unions from gaining the power unions had in Europe. However, organized labor did make some gains. By 1904, union membership in America stood at two million workers. The AFL accounted for most of these people. Samuel Gompers's belief in "bread-and-butter unionism" proved to be effective for its time, and under his leadership, labor unions came to be accepted by some Americans.

Today, we celebrate the labor movement in America on Labor Day. Each year, on the first Monday in September, we acknowledge the achievements and efforts of American workers. Labor Day began in the late 1800s, and became a federal holiday in 1894.

Although the strike at the Carnegie steel plant in Homestead, Pennsylvania, was not successful, over time, labor unions became an accepted part of the industrialized age.

Chapter 9
The Urbanization of America

Growing Cities During the late 1800s and early 1900s, American cities experienced extraordinary growth. A few cities grew to become some of the largest in the world.

The Big Question

Why did many American cities grow so rapidly during the early 1900s?

New York's population, which was already more than one million in 1860, soared to 4.7 million by 1910. Philadelphia went from nearly half a million to one million people in that same time. Chicago's population rose from about one hundred thousand to more than two million.

Some of these changes took place with breathtaking speed. During the 1880s alone, the size of some cities doubled and even tripled. Kansas City, Missouri, went from 60,000 to 132,000, and Minneapolis, Minnesota, from 47,000 to 164,000. Places like Birmingham, Alabama, and Duluth, Minnesota, were small towns in 1880 and busy cities by 1890.

Although at the end of the century, it was still true that more Americans lived in rural areas than in cities—twice as many, in fact—no one could doubt where the future led. The United States was fast becoming a nation of city dwellers.

By the beginning of the 1900s, there were two million people living in Chicago.
Here you can see a busy street in Chicago at this time.

Railroads and Cities

It was no coincidence that this remarkable **urban** growth occurred when railroad companies were creating a web of tracks across the land. Most of these cities were centers of transportation. Some

of the largest were New York, Philadelphia, and Baltimore on the East Coast; San Francisco on the West Coast; and New Orleans on the Gulf of Mexico. What did they all have in common? They were older cities whose fine harbors had given them their start. A few—St. Louis, Missouri, and Buffalo, New York—owed their growth to the rivers or canals they were located on. But it was the railroad as much as anything else that allowed these places to become huge urban areas by 1900. And it was the railroad that turned many small towns into bustling cities.

Minneapolis, Minnesota, for example, had always had good water transportation, as well as the falls of the Mississippi River. But that city did not boom until railroads connected it to the wheat lands of the West and made it a center for milling flour. Chicago, on Lake Michigan, experienced its greatest growth when it became the connecting point for eastern and western railroads.

Perhaps the most spectacular example of how railroads turned towns into cities was Kansas City, Missouri. Kansas City was a small town of four thousand people in 1860. Located on a great bend of the Missouri River, it was a loading and unloading area for steamboats headed east or west. Nearby was the town of Leavenworth, Kansas, with a population of about eight thousand. An army fort was located close by, and Leavenworth's merchants did a thriving business with the fort's soldiers. Leavenworth was also a supply center on the main wagon route to the West. Had you asked anyone at that time which of these two cities they expected to grow faster, the answer would have been, "Leavenworth, for sure."

But that is not what happened. Leavenworth did grow a bit, but it never became a really large city. That honor went to Kansas City, and it was all because several railroad companies decided to build their main lines through that city rather than through Leavenworth. These railroads connected Kansas City to the farming and cattle country farther west, and to Chicago, St. Louis, and other cities in the North and East.

Before long, business boomed in Kansas City. Flour mills sprang up to process wheat from Kansas and Nebraska, and new meatpacking plants handled cattle from the Great Plains. Between 1860 and 1880, the population of Kansas City grew from four thousand to fifty thousand people. Twenty years later its population reached 160,000.

Cattle could be transported by train to Kansas City from ranches farther west.

Manufacturing and Cities

Along with the railroad, manufacturing contributed mightily to the growth of America's cities in the second half of the 1800s. The earliest machines, you will remember, were driven by waterpower. That meant the factories had to be built next to rivers and streams.

By the 1840s and 1850s, however, manufacturers began switching to steam engines to power their machines. That freed businessmen to build their factories anywhere they wanted. Most chose to build in cities. Why was this the case? Cities had what manufacturers needed: good transportation, plenty of workers, and a lot of customers for their products.

Some cities owed their growth to a single large industry. Pittsburgh, Pennsylvania, and Birmingham, Alabama, became centers for making steel. Minneapolis, Minnesota, and Kansas City, Missouri, grew as centers for milling wheat. Very large cities like New York, Chicago, and Philadelphia, of course, had many different industries. These cities also grew because of their importance as centers for transportation and banking, supplying the money needed by manufacturers across the country.

New City Dwellers

And so the cities grew. In 1860, about six million people lived in America's cities. In 1900, some thirty million did. Where did these millions of new city dwellers come from? Urban populations came mainly from two sources.

One was America's countryside. Between 1880 and 1910, about eleven million Americans gave up farming and moved to the city. In some parts of New England and the Midwest, entire villages were abandoned.

One reason for this was that during most of the late 1800s, prices for farm products kept dropping. Many farmers had large debts. The drop in farm prices meant they could not pay their debts, and they lost their farms. Some stayed to work on land that now belonged to others.

Many others, though, decided that if they could no longer work their own land, they might as well move to the city. A man could earn several hundred dollars more a year working in someone else's factory than he could earn by working on someone else's farm.

For some, the city seemed a place of glamour and excitement in comparison to an isolated farm where the days could feel quite lonely. It was a place where gas and, after Thomas Edison, electric streetlights turned night into day.

Compared to life on a farm, or in a small town, life in a big city—such as New York City (shown here)—seemed very appealing to some.

Where but in a city could you listen to all kinds of music or hear talks by famous people? Where but in a city could you encounter the wonders of the modern age: department stores with their hundreds of goods on display, the ice box that kept dairy foods fresh even during the heat of summer, and that wonder of wonders, indoor plumbing?

Even more, the city was a place of opportunity. Schools and libraries offered the chance for education and new careers. Hundreds of different kinds of jobs were available, and possibly, even fame and fortune.

The second great source of new city dwellers was the huge tide of immigration, mostly from Europe. More than three of every four immigrants wound up in America's growing cities. These immigrants were a major source of labor for the city's factories.

Another part of the story of migration to the cities is that of the newly emancipated (freed) African American worker. When slavery was abolished in 1865, some African Americans ventured north to the expanding cities of Cleveland, Philadelphia, New York, Boston, and Chicago. There men, women, and children sought work in much the same way newly arrived immigrants did. In the beginning this migration was gradual, but by the early part of the 1900s, thousands of African American workers had moved north to work on the railroads, in the factories, and to set up businesses of their own.

Upward and Outward

As America's cities grew, they spread both upward and outward. The rapid increase in population had caused land prices in cities to skyrocket. In some large cities, land that could have sold for a hundred dollars in the 1840s cost a hundred thousand dollars forty years later. Builders found it cheaper to build upward than to build outward. Even before the Civil War, five- and six-story buildings lined the streets of a few of America's larger cities.

However, there was a limit to how high a building could be. The problem in those days was that the whole weight of a building, including the floors and the inner walls, was supported by its outside walls. To build tall buildings, the walls had to be very thick. As a result, few office buildings could be more than five or six stories high.

In 1884, an architect named William Le Baron Jenney figured out the secret to building taller buildings: build a steel skeleton to carry the weight of the building, and make the outer walls simply a covering for it. The next year, in 1885, Jenney completed a ten-story building for an insurance company in Chicago. The development of the electric elevator at about the same time was the final step needed to usher in the age of the **skyscraper**, a uniquely American invention.

> **Vocabulary**
>
> **skyscraper,** n.
> an extremely tall building

At about the same time, cities began to spread outward. Before the Civil War, all American cities were "walking cities"—that is, most people got around them on foot. Because that included getting to and from work, a walking city almost never spread more than two miles from its center in any direction, about the distance someone might walk in a half hour. Houses were mixed together with factories, warehouses, offices, and stores, and rich and poor never lived far from each other. When the population of a walking city increased, more people simply crowded into the same space.

New developments in transportation, however, began to change the walking city. The first of these was the horse-drawn street railway, or horse car, that made its appearance in the mid-1800s. Drawn along tracks in the center of

Here you can see a horse car on a Boston street in the early 1900s.

the street, horse cars carried people about twice as fast as they could walk. That meant that those who could afford the fare could now live three or four miles from work and still get there in half an hour. The city began to spread out.

Starting in the 1880s, several new forms of transportation changed the shape of the American city. In 1887, Frank J. Sprague designed and built an electric street railway, or trolley car, in Richmond, Virginia. The trolley car carried people nearly twice as fast as horse cars. The trolley car was so obviously superior that in hardly more than ten years it had replaced the horse car in nearly every American city. Meanwhile, in New York, enterprising businessmen built elevated railroads. The trains on these "els" rode on tracks high above the city streets. The tracks were supported by steel posts.

Underground city railroads called **subways** were also designed and built. America's first subway opened in Boston in 1897.

These transportation developments allowed the city to spread out still farther. By 1900, a large city might measure eight or ten miles from one end to the other. This helped relieve the overcrowding of the inner cities. At the same time, however, it led to a different kind of problem: the separation of the wealthy from the poor. Those who could afford the new housing that was built along the streetcar and train lines moved away from the city center. Left behind in the older neighborhoods near the factories, docks, and warehouses were the poor people and the newcomers to the city who worked there. This separation of rich and poor would turn out to be only one of the growing problems of the American city.

> **Vocabulary**
> ....
> **subway,** n. an underground train system

Developments in city transportation made it possible for large numbers of people to move around a city more easily. The photograph at the top of the page shows rush hour in Washington, D.C., in 1920. The photograph below shows an elevated train line in New York City in 1903.

Chapter 10
Growing Pains

Urban Problems As America's cities grew in the late 1800s, urban problems grew as well. One of the most severe problems was housing. As you may remember, in most large cities, housing was terribly inadequate. New York, the nation's largest city, had the worst housing problem.

The Big Question

Why do you think this chapter is called "growing pains"?

In the older parts of the city, residents packed into apartment buildings called tenements. Tenement rooms often had little direct light or air. Usually there was no running water either; tenants had to take buckets to a public pump in the street to get water for cooking or bathing.

Most people who lived in tenements were poor, so to help pay the rent, they often took in **boarders**. Of course that made the already crowded buildings still more crowded. One five-story tenement at 36 Cherry Street, in New York, was already filled up in 1865 when it housed five hundred people. Twelve years later, there were eight hundred people crammed into that same building.

Vocabulary

boarder, n. a person who pays to rent a room and receive meals

As New York's population grew, builders constructed more tenements. In 1880, more than half a million New Yorkers lived in tenements. By 1900, that number had climbed to one and a half million people. Similar situations existed in other large cities.

People who moved to the crowded cities and lived in tenements hoped to one day be able to move out and have a better standard of living.

What a Mess!

Cities could not keep up with the demand for the most basic services. Take street paving, for example. In 1890, two-thirds of the streets in Chicago, the nation's second-largest city, remained unpaved. In that same year, four-fifths of New Orleans's five hundred miles of street were still dirt, while not a single one of Minneapolis's two hundred miles of streets was paved. Only a few cities, such as Buffalo, Washington, D.C., Boston, and New York, could boast about having well-paved streets by the end of the 1800s. Everywhere else, walkers and riders got around as best they could on dusty—or when it rained, muddy—streets.

Garbage disposal was another problem that few cities dealt with effectively. Even in those days, Americans were creating more trash than any other people in the world. At the turn of the century, an American city dweller produced an average of 860 pounds of trash per year, nearly twice as much as a person living in an English city.

What to do with all that garbage? Some coastal cities got rid of it by loading it onto barges and dumping it into the ocean. In a few cities, farmers were paid to haul the garbage away and feed it to their pigs. In most cities, however, people got rid of their garbage just as they always had. They threw it into the streets and alleys, where it was eaten by pigs that roamed the streets.

Disposing of sewage (human waste) was a greater problem. Family outhouses (outdoor toilets) and cesspools (underground catch-basins for human waste) had been used when the population was small. With hundreds of people now living in a single city building, these older methods of handling human waste would no longer do. As late as the 1890s, some cities still dumped sewage into open gutters and waited for rain to wash it away.

A number of cities built underground sewer systems to carry the sewage away. That was fine, except that these systems carried sewage to nearby rivers that were often the source of a city's drinking water. Every day,

New York City was one of the first cities in America to have an underground sewer system. This photograph was taken in 1911. In the photograph you can see two workers employed to work in the sewers that run beneath the city streets.

Philadelphia's sewer system dumped thirteen million gallons of sewage into the Delaware River, the city's main water source. Not surprisingly, such waterborne diseases as typhoid fever and cholera spread quickly and took the lives of thousands. Children were especially at risk, and the death rate among infants was terrible. Half the children born in Chicago in the 1880s did not live to the age of five.

Perhaps the worst urban problem was fire. It is a problem that has plagued large towns and cities from the time they first began to develop. Older buildings in American cities were made of wood, and they were crowded closely together. A single spark might start a fire that could burn down an entire neighborhood. One of the worst fires of the century occurred in Chicago in 1871. Within days, a third of the city—seventeen thousand buildings—was destroyed, leaving three hundred dead and ninety thousand homeless. The next year a large part of Boston also went up in flames.

Finally, there was the growing problem of crime. Robbery, assault, and murder were on the rise. Some young people joined street gangs that terrorized citizens. Police refused to enter some sections of New York, San Francisco, and a few other cities.

This image shows people fleeing the Great Chicago Fire of 1871.

By the end of the century, many cities were tackling these problems that came with urban growth. City governments stopped depending on volunteer firemen and hired full-time, trained men for the job. They developed professional police forces. They hired companies to pave streets, build schools, collect garbage, improve sewage systems, and provide city dwellers with clean drinking water.

The Political Machine

Catching up with the needs of a growing city meant spending money—a lot of it. This money came from **taxes**, money raised by taxing people and businesses. The builder hired to put up a new school or courthouse would make hundreds or even thousands of dollars. The company that got the contract to pave streets or build a sewage system would make even more. A trolley company that gained permission to put tracks down the center of city streets stood to make millions of dollars in fares over the years. Who would decide which companies got the jobs? City officials, some elected and some appointed, did.

It was a situation ready-made for **corruption**. Companies would gladly give thousands of dollars in **payoffs** to city officials to get the job and make millions in profits. And there were always some officials who would gladly take them.

Into this situation stepped the **political machine** and the **political boss**. The machine decided who would be the party's candidates for election and then got them elected. Once elected, the officials took their orders from the boss. The boss saw to it that contracts were awarded to the "right" people, the ones who paid off the machine.

Most large cities in the late 1800s had political machines and bosses. Few, however, operated with the boldness and openness of William Marcy Tweed. Tweed was the boss in the late 1860s and 1870s of an organization called Tammany Hall that for decades controlled the Democratic Party in New York City. In just three years, Tweed and his gang stole $100 million from the city government through

In this cartoon created by Thomas Nast in 1872, William Marcy Tweed is shown as being above "the arm of the law."

such trickery as billing the city $11 million for a new courthouse that cost just $3 million to build. Tweed finally went to jail, but Tammany Hall continued its raid of New York's treasury.

Most machine politicians enriched themselves by more subtle means than the open thievery of "Boss Tweed." Their main method was using political power and bribes to get city business, such as garbage collection, or to fix elections. They might, for example, obtain secret payments from companies to which they awarded construction contracts. One such politician, a man named George Washington Plunkett, explained a favorite method of his own, which he called "honest graft":

> My party's in power in the city, and it's goin' to undertake a lot of public improvements. Well, I'm tipped off, say, that they're going to lay out a new park at a certain place. I see my opportunity and I take it. I go to that place and I buy up all the land I can in the neighborhood. Then the board of this or that makes its plan public, and there is a rush to get my land, which nobody cared particular for before. Ain't it perfectly honest to charge a good price and make a profit on my investment and foresight? Of course, it is. Well, that's honest graft. . . . It's just like lookin' ahead in Wall Street or in the coffee and cotton market. It's honest graft, and I'm lookin' for it every day of the year.

Plunkett suggested that when he died, his tombstone should read: "He Seen His Opportunities, and He Took 'Em."

One of the reasons a political machine was able to elect "its people" was because it won the support of the immigrants who poured into American cities. When immigrants arrived in America, except for help from family members and fellow countrymen, they were on their own. There were no government programs of any kind to help them get settled in the city.

The political machine saw an opportunity and seized it. The machine helped immigrants at the docks by meeting them as they came off the boats. The machine helped the immigrants find jobs and places to live. It gave the immigrants food and coal in hard times. It joined their celebrations, attended their weddings, and comforted them at their funerals.

The political machine also helped immigrants become American citizens so they could vote. In return, grateful immigrants voted for the machine's candidates on Election Day. To the immigrants, that seemed a fair exchange. Unfortunately, their votes also made it possible for people like George Washington Plunkett to do the things he did.

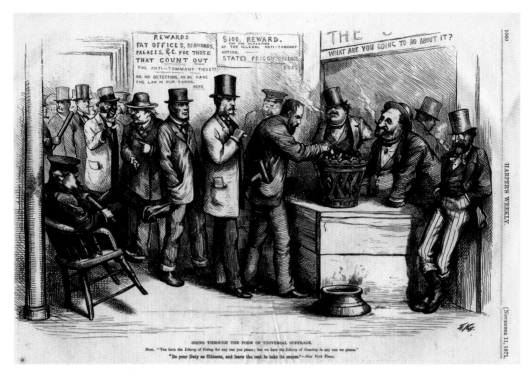

GOING THROUGH THE FORM OF UNIVERSAL SUFFRAGE.

Boss. "You have the *Liberty of Voting* for any one you please ; but we have the *Liberty of Counting* in any one we please."

"Do your Duty as Citizens, and leave the rest to take its course."—*New York Times.*

The clear message in this cartoon is that the results of elections in many cities were dishonest because some people voted under pressure from others.

Built on Immigrants

As you have already discovered, so much of the story of the industrial development of America, including its financial, political, and social successes, could not have happened without a labor force made up of not only Americans, but also of people from all over the world. Very often, these people came to America with very little. They worked hard, made new lives for themselves, and contributed greatly to the development of their adopted home. The story of the immigrant is a powerful one. They were in many ways great adventurers who set off unsure of what lay ahead but willing to face all kinds of challenges. They left their mark in the skyscrapers of New York and Chicago, in the railroads, tunnels, and bridges that cross this vast land, in their inventions and innovations that changed the world, and in their belief in America's greatness.

Immigrant Gallery

These photographs are of immigrants who arrived at Ellis Island, New York, in the early 1900s.

Immigrants arriving at Ellis Island, 1902

Immigrants arriving in New York City, 1905

Immigrants eating a meal on Ellis Island, 1906

Immigrants arriving at Ellis Island, 1910

A child about to set foot on Ellis Island, 1926

Immigrants meeting an official at Ellis Island, 1928

Immigrants ready to leave Ellis Island, 1929

Glossary

A

accounting, n. the process of recording, summarizing, and analyzing business transactions (116)

anarchist, n. a person who rebels against or works to disrupt an established authority, usually a government or an economic system (121)

B

blacklist, v. to list people or groups in order to avoid or exclude them (123)

boarder, n. a person who pays to rent a room and receive meals (138)

C

capital, n. money needed to pay for a workforce, machinery, and other equipment to support the development and growth of a business (75)

carbon, n. a nonmetal substance that makes up diamonds and graphite and is found in coal (84)

combustion engine, n. an engine that converts fuel, such as gasoline, to energy (81)

commerce, n. the buying and selling of goods and services; trade (107)

consumption, n. a disease that causes the body to waste away, generally over a long period of time; tuberculosis (115)

convenience, n. something that makes life easier or more comfortable (118)

corporation, n. a type of company, usually made up of many people, with certain legal rights and protections to conduct business (75)

corruption, n. illegal or dishonest behavior, often by people in a position of power (143)

crude oil, n. naturally occurring oil that has not been processed to remove impurities (95)

E

efficient, adj. productive without wasting time or resources (93)

electric current, n. the flow of electricity through a circuit (84)

engineer, n. a person who uses science and math to build useful objects or buildings (116)

enterprise, n. an organized activity meant to make a profit; a company (90)

F

"federal government," (phrase) a national government that shares power with state or regional governments (64)

free enterprise, n. a system in which businesses operate with minimal government involvement (107)

freight, n. shipped goods; cargo (100)

G

garment, n. an article of clothing (113)

I

impurity, n. an unwanted substance that makes something impure or contaminated (90)

industrialism, n. the organization of society around an economy based on the use of machines and factories (67)

investor, n. a person who puts money into a business with the goal of later making a profit (55)

M

machinist, n. a person who operates, designs, builds, or fixes machines (116)

manufacturer, n. a person or company that makes or produces an item to be sold (57)

market economy, n. an economic system in which prices are determined by competition among businesses and not by the government (69)

mass production, n. the making of very large amounts of something (111)

mineral, n. a naturally occurring substance found in Earth's crust (72)

monopoly, n. complete ownership or control of a resource or industry (102)

N

natural resource, n. something from nature that is useful to humans (72)

O

ore, n. rock from which metal can be obtained (72)

P

patent, n. a license from the government that gives the person requesting the patent the exclusive right to make, use, or sell an invention (78)

payoff, n. a bribe (143)

phonograph, n. a machine that records and reproduces sound; a record player (83)

"political boss," (phrase), the leader of a political machine (143)

"political machine," (phrase), a group that maintains political control, usually of a city, through bribery and intimidation (143)

R

refinery, n. a place where resources are processed, usually for industrial use (95)

regulate, v. to control or place limits on (105)

S

skyscraper, n. an extremely tall building (134)

socialism, n. an economic system in which major industries are owned or regulated by the government, rather than by private businesses (120)

"spinning mill," (phrase) a factory that makes thread or yarn (59)

"standard time zone," (phrase) an area within which everyone observes the same time (70)

subway, n. an underground train system (136)

sweatshop, n. a factory in which employees work for long hours in unsafe conditions for a low wage (113)

T

tax, n. money that people must pay to the government so that it can fund such things as schools and roads (143)

telegraph, n. a machine that communicates messages over long distances by sending signals through wires (54)

textile, n. cloth or fabric (55)

ton, n. a unit of weight equal to two thousand pounds (66)

transcontinental, adj. across a continent (64)

trust, n. a combination of corporations created to reduce competition and control prices (102)

trustee, n. an individual responsible for overseeing a trust (102)

U

union, n. an organization formed by workers to win and protect workers' rights (120)

urban, adj. relating to a city (130)

W

weaver, n. a person who makes fabric by weaving threads or yarn together (52)

Reform in Industrial America

Table of Contents

Reader

Core Knowledge History and Geography™

Chapter 1
The Populist Movement

An Age of Extremes At the end of the 1800s, the number of people living in the United States had grown to more than 76 million. More than 14 million immigrants had moved to the United States between 1860 and 1900. Most of the people arriving from other countries flooded into the cities. Many immigrants, including children, found jobs in factories. Factory workers toiled for long hours, often in dangerous conditions, to earn small amounts of money.

The Big Question

What was the populist movement, and what were their main concerns?

On the other hand, the owners of large businesses and great railroads became millionaires. Politicians worked together with the wealthy and powerful, and resisted making laws that would be unpopular with these influential people.

Vocabulary

segregation, n. the act of keeping people separate, usually on the basis of race

While many people who were not rich lived comfortably, many others lived difficult, challenging lives. Farmers struggled to survive. City dwellers lived crowded together in unsafe apartment buildings. Minorities, especially African Americans, faced racial **segregation** and discrimination. Women could not vote. The time was ripe for changes in the system—for reform.

Reform was needed to protect men, women, and children who worked long hours, often in unsafe conditions, in factories.

Discontent Among Farmers

One area where the demand for reform began was in the formation of a new **political party**, the **Populist** Party. American farmers formed the Populist Party in 1891, but the seeds that led to this new party had been planted decades before.

In the 1880s, American farmers seemed to have many advantages. Many owned vast farms, large herds, and modern farm equipment that was the envy of the rest of the world. But as the farmers raised more grain and livestock, the prices of these products dropped. Many crops lost half their value within ten years. At the same time, railroad shipping costs for carrying the crops to market went up.

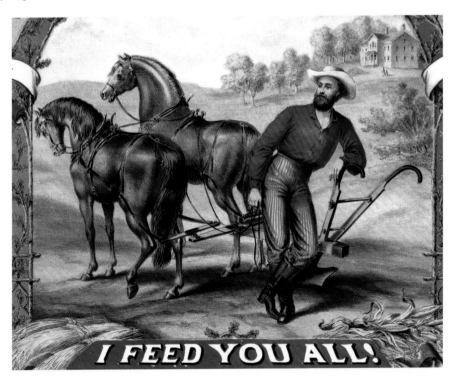

I FEED YOU ALL!

This image shows a piece of art that was inspired by the Granger movement, an organization set up by mostly Midwestern farmers. The image shows the importance of farming, and the belief that the railroad companies and big businesses were hurting farmers.

The situation was especially bad in the West and Southwest. Droughts in the Great Plains caused many farmers to leave their farms to return to the East. One observer described a parade of defeated farmers who had given up on farming: "The discouraged settlers trekked out of the drought-stricken country. Day after day they passed by, grizzled, dejected, and surly men; sick, tired, and hopeless women."

Drought was not the only problem for farmers. They were also plagued by grasshoppers so ravenously hungry that they ate the paint on the wagons, chewed through saddles, and left holes in the kitchen curtains. Dust storms, floods, tornadoes, fires, and thieves—all these were constant threats to the farmers' livelihood. Combined with the drop in prices for their crops, these calamities finally got the better of the farmers' spirits. People in difficult situations like these often seek someone to blame. In this case, anger was directed toward the supply of money in the United States.

Gold Standard Versus Free Silver

The farmers believed that the banks' tight control over the availability of money was one reason for their troubles. This whole idea is pretty complicated. If you look at a dollar bill, you will see the words FEDERAL RESERVE NOTE printed across the top. But these words were not always there. Not so long ago, the words SILVER CERTIFICATE appeared on the dollar bill. Early dollar bills also contained this announcement:

THIS CERTIFIES THAT THERE HAS BEEN DEPOSITED

IN THE TREASURY OF

THE UNITED STATES OF AMERICA

ONE SILVER DOLLAR

PAYABLE TO THE BEARER ON DEMAND

That meant that you could go into a bank and trade your dollar bill for a dollar's worth of silver. Before silver certificates were issued, gold certificates carried the same message.

This silver certificate features Martha Washington, who was married to George Washington. It is the only example of a woman's portrait on U.S. paper money.

During the Civil War, the U.S. government issued greenbacks, or paper currency, to help pay for the war. (Our paper money today is still green, the color that gave greenbacks their name.) But having more paper money around led to **inflation**, so things cost more than they had a year before.

Then the government decided it did not want so many dollars in circulation because an oversupply of money meant that its value decreased. As the government decreased the money supply, it became harder and harder to get hold of dollars.

This tight supply of money hurt farmers who were in debt. Many of them had borrowed money to buy machinery or to buy more land so they could plant more crops. The farmers signed loan contracts, called mortgages, with the banks. The mortgages said that if the farmers did not repay their loans on time, the banks could take the farms. As crops failed, the farmers could not earn enough money to repay their loans.

People were not sure whether they could trust paper money to be worth as much as money made of metal. One reason was that the gold that backed up the paper money was in short supply. How had this happened? As the population had grown, the demand for gold had also grown. At the same time, gold mines weren't producing as much gold as they had in the past. As the gold supply decreased, many people could no longer trade their dollars in for gold. Meanwhile, silver mines were producing more and more silver. There was plenty of silver that could be turned into coins, but the value of silver could vary more than the value of gold, which worried the bankers who loaned large sums of money. They were concerned that the banks would earn less money from their investments.

The People's Party

The farmers wanted the government to start using silver for money. Those who wanted the government to rely on silver were known as supporters of "free silver." Many of the farmers who supported free silver also wanted relief from the low prices they got for their products and from the high prices they paid the railroads to ship these products. These angry farmers joined together with some unhappy **trade union** members to form the Populist Party.

> **Vocabulary**
> ....
> **trade union,** n. an organization formed by workers with a specific skill, such as electricians, to win and protect their rights; today the term is used interchangeably with *labor union*

People who joined the new party were called Populists, but so were nonparty members who wanted political change in certain areas. The Populists wanted more than free silver. Their demands also included a shorter workday and a graduated income tax. With a graduated income tax, wealthy people pay a higher percentage of their income in taxes than those who earn less, such as farmers and factory workers.

Of course, there were two sides to the great currency debate, as there usually are. On one side of the issue were western farmers who supported the free silver policy. On the other side were eastern bankers who wanted paper money to be backed by gold, not silver. These bankers still had access to plenty of gold. They felt that gold should remain the standard. These supporters of the **gold standard** were sometimes called "gold bugs." Many of the people who were in favor of the gold standard would also have to pay more taxes if a graduated income tax were to become law. Into this bitterly divided political situation stepped one of the greatest public speakers in American history, William Jennings Bryan.

William Jennings Bryan

Imagine a time before television, movies, computers, or even radio. What might you do for fun? It may surprise you that a popular pastime in the 1800s and early 1900s was going to hear people give speeches. In fact, in high schools throughout the United States, students competed and received prizes for their ability to recite poems and essays. The art of speaking in public is called oratory. Public speeches are called orations. Oratory was a highly prized skill in the late 1800s, before electricity was available to spur the invention of the forms of entertainment we enjoy today.

William Jennings Bryan, born in 1860, was practically an orator from birth. As soon as he learned to read, Bryan would climb up on a table and from memory recite his lessons to his mother.

When he was about your age, Bryan went with his father to a political convention. There, after listening to the speakers, the boy took the stage. The audience smiled, amused by the youngster who was so sure of himself. But as the boy spoke, they listened intently and then cheered wildly and carried him around the room when he finished.

His talent as an orator brought William Jennings Bryan to prominence. As the 1896 election approached, members of the Democratic Party were looking for a candidate to run for president. They wanted someone who supported their cause of free silver. Bryan had built a reputation as a brilliant debater while he was still a boy, and then again as a student at Illinois College. He had also served two terms in the House of Representatives. Bryan was just the man the Democrats needed to run for president. He was well spoken, well liked, and a supporter of free silver.

The Democratic Convention

As a candidate, Bryan was the first politician to travel widely, using public-speaking appearances to attract followers. As he traveled, the great orator tried out some phrases in his speeches. Two phrases, "cross of gold" and "crown of thorns," had been warmly received by his listeners. These ideas used language from the Bible, which was familiar to Bryan's audience. He discovered that the mixture of religion and politics that came naturally to him was a hit with many Americans.

In William Shakespeare's play *Julius Caesar*, two characters debate whether the assassination of Caesar was justified. Brutus speaks first and wins support from the audience, but then Marc Antony gives an even better speech and completely wins over the crowd. Shakespeare's play shows that the last speaker in a debate can have a big advantage, provided he has the necessary public-speaking skills. In a debate at the 1896 Democratic Convention over whether the silver issue would become central in the upcoming election, Bryan had the opportunity to speak last, and—like Marc Antony—he used it to his advantage.

"Cross of Gold" Speech

Bryan wanted to make the issue of free silver central to the presidential campaign. He had to convince skeptical Democrats to this point of view. He trusted that his "Cross of Gold" speech would not fail him.

Bryan began by defending farmers and working people:

> The man who is employed for wages is as much a businessman as his employer; . . . the farmer who goes forth in the morning and toils all day—who begins in the spring and toils all summer—and who by the application of brain and muscle to the natural resources of the country creates wealth, is as much a businessman as the man who goes upon the board of trade and bets upon the price of grain; the miners who go down a thousand feet into the earth, or climb two thousand feet upon the cliffs, and bring forth from their hiding places the precious metals to be poured into the channels of trade are as much businessmen as the few financial magnates [wealthy and powerful bankers] who, in a back room, corner the money of the world.
>
> We come to speak for this broader class of businessmen. . . . There are two ideas of government. There are those who believe that, if you will only legislate [make laws] to make the well-to-do prosperous, their prosperity will leak through on those below. The Democratic idea, however, has been that if you legislate to make the masses prosperous, their prosperity will find its way up through every class which rests upon them.

Then Bryan turned to the gold standard:

> You come to us and tell us that the great cities are in favor of the gold standard; we reply that the great cities rest upon our broad and fertile prairies. Burn down your cities and leave our farms, and your cities will spring up again as if by magic; but destroy our farms and the grass will grow in the streets of every city in the country.

Even before he finished, it was clear that Bryan's speech was a hit. Bryan later recalled, "The audience seemed to rise and sit down as one man. At the close of a sentence it would rise and shout, and when I began upon another sentence the room was still as a church."

But it was Bryan's final lines that really brought down the house. With his audience completely under his spell, Bryan delivered the closing words that were guaranteed to get the response he wanted:

> You shall not press down upon the brow of labor this crown of thorns, you shall not crucify mankind upon a cross of gold!

When the speech ended, there was silence. Then came deafening cheers. The audience took Bryan onto their shoulders and carried him around. It took thirty-five minutes to restore calm. The next day, Bryan was chosen to run for president on the Democratic Party ticket. The great orator earned more than the nomination of the Democratic Party. He was not only the candidate of the Populists, he was the champion of the free silver movement.

William Jennings Bryan's skill as a public speaker won him the Democratic nomination in 1896.

Effects of Populism

Bryan did not win the election of 1896. However, he made a good showing against the Republican candidate, William McKinley. In time, McKinley and his vice president, Theodore Roosevelt, would adopt many populist ideas.

As the economy improved under the Republicans, the issue of free silver became a thing of the past. It was no longer a concern for farmers. Other issues raised by the Populists had been absorbed by the Democrats. And the Republican Party had also addressed several reform issues. The workday was shortened, and an income tax amendment was passed in 1913.

Noted primarily for his "Cross of Gold" speech, an issue that simply no longer mattered, Bryan also lost the presidential elections in 1900 and 1908. However, he served as **secretary of state** from 1913 to 1915 under President Woodrow Wilson.

> **Vocabulary**
>
> **secretary of state,** n. the U.S. government official in charge of helping the president in his dealings with foreign countries

William Jennings Bryan, born in Salem, Illinois, in 1860, was a wonderful public speaker.

Chapter 2
The Muckrakers

The Haves and Have-Nots By 1900, the United States was the most industrialized nation in the world. At this time, the mighty business leaders and captains of industry were as powerful as kings. You may have read about some of these men—men such as Andrew Carnegie, J.P. Morgan, Cornelius Vanderbilt, and John D. Rockefeller.

The Big Question

Why were some journalists at this time called "muckrakers," and why was their work important?

The general public got most of their news from newspapers. Newspapers were sold on the street and in stores. Quite often people bought a newspaper on their way to work.

There were few checks on these business leaders. The federal government did little to interfere with their ambition. There were few laws governing the way they conducted business.

A number of journalists felt that these business leaders were abusing their power. The journalists wanted to make the public aware of these suspected abuses. They wrote articles exposing the secret inner workings of big business. Newspapers and magazines found a growing audience across the nation for these kinds of articles. The journalists who wrote these articles became known as "muckrakers." A muckraker was a journalist who would dig up "dirt." In doing so, the muckraker would uncover all kinds of stories.

Muckraking

A muckrake was originally the name for a tool, like a pitchfork, that was used to clean out barns and stables. When Theodore Roosevelt first used the term *muckrake* in 1906 to describe the work of certain journalists, he did not mean it as a compliment. He referred to one investigative journalist as "the Man with the Muckrake . . . who could look no way but downward," meaning that this man was always looking for dirt to uncover.

However, the work of muckrakers and other social reformers would lead to many improvements in the lives of average Americans. Indeed, so many changes were made during this period that it became known as the **Progressive Era**.

Various muckrakers gained praise and recognition for uncovering the "dirty" side of **capitalism**. Two of the best-known muckrakers, Ida Tarbell and Upton Sinclair, were associated with particular industries. Tarbell is noted for exposing a company

> ### Vocabulary
>
> **"Progressive Era,"** (phrase) a time of social and political activism in the United States during the early 1900s, characterized by changes and reforms aimed at improving people's lives
>
> **capitalism,** n. an economic system in which resources and businesses are privately owned and prices are not controlled by the government

called Standard Oil. Sinclair is known for his work describing the **meatpacking** industry.

Ida Tarbell

In 1869, when Ida Tarbell was twelve, her family moved to Titusville, Pennsylvania. Her father, Franklin, was an independent oilman who made barrels used in the **oil-refining** business. He joined other oilmen who tried—unsuccessfully— to fight John D. Rockefeller's takeover of oil production in Pennsylvania. Rockefeller's company, Standard Oil, was on its way to becoming the largest oil company in the country. Rockefeller was becoming one of America's richest individuals. Rockefeller controlled the pipelines that carried the oil from the wells to the refineries. He also controlled the refineries and factories where the oil found in the ground—known as crude oil—was turned into useful products. Soon many of his competitors found themselves out of business, unable to compete with Rockefeller.

Franklin and Esther Tarbell raised four children. The eldest was Ida Minerva. She was named for a character in literature who supported higher education for women (Ida) and for the Roman goddess of wisdom (Minerva). Ida's mother, a supporter of women's rights, was determined that Ida would try to imitate her namesakes by pursuing wisdom and education.

Although Ida Tarbell's father did not support his daughter's desire for an education, he agreed to let her enroll at nearby Allegheny College. She was the only woman among the forty students in her class. After graduating from college, she worked as an editor at a local newspaper. She worked there until her boss put his nineteen-year-old son in charge of the paper one summer. Ida, who was thirty-three, was angered. She left in protest. She went to France, to study French history and to write.

While she was in Paris, Ida Tarbell wrote an article on an unlikely topic: the paving of Parisian streets. She sent this article to a new American magazine called *McClure's* magazine. Publisher Samuel McClure's instant response was, "This girl can write." He hired Tarbell immediately and urged her to come home from France and join his staff as an associate editor.

This is the front cover of an edition of *McClure's* magazine published in the 1910s.

Tarbell at *McClure's* Magazine

McClure could not have made a better choice. In only a few months, Tarbell's articles helped increase the number of readers from 40,000 a month to 250,000. *McClure's* became the most popular magazine in the United States, in part because of Tarbell.

Tarbell was also a hit with the magazine's staff. A coworker at the magazine had nothing but praise for her: "She is beautiful with virtue—so generous, so modest, so full of kindness, so able, so gallant—and yet with such good sense and humor."

Ida Tarbell wrote on many different topics. She always brought a sense of fairness to her writing. After writing biographies of Napoleon Bonaparte and Abraham Lincoln, Tarbell was assigned to write a series of articles on the workings of the Standard Oil Company.

Government Policy

John D. Rockefeller, owner of the Standard Oil Company, was a wealthy, powerful businessman who was used to getting his own way. In 1878, Rockefeller controlled more than 90 percent of oil production in the United States. He was so successful that many of his competitors were going out of business. In fact, that was part of Rockefeller's plan.

In 1890, the Sherman Antitrust Act was passed in Congress. This law was designed to keep large companies and powerful industrialists from interfering

John D. Rockefeller was a powerful and highly successful businessman who did not take no for an answer.

with **free trade** or limiting competition. At the time, large **trusts** controlled major industries. The trusts were groups of related companies within an industry, all controlled by a single governing board.

The new law was intended to keep the giant trusts from putting small companies out of business. It was supposed to prevent one company, or a group of cooperating companies, from controlling an entire industry. But the Sherman Antitrust Act did not achieve the desired result. In fact, after the law was passed, twenty-five new trusts were formed. Instead of protecting small businesses from giant trusts, the law was used to crush union efforts at labor reform.

> **Vocabulary**
>
> **free trade,** n. a policy of unrestricted trade, in which the government does not use quotas, tariffs, or other measures to regulate imports and exports
>
> **trust,** n. a combination of corporations created to reduce competition and control prices

Standard Oil Trust

Rockefeller's Standard Oil Company was the first trust. It was also one of the most powerful trusts. One of the ways that the company had been able to get rich was through the use of rebates. You may know of rebates as money you get back from a manufacturer for buying a certain product. Around 1900, a rebate was a little different. It was more like what we call a "kickback," or bribe, today.

Here's how the rebates worked. Standard Oil shipped its product by railroad. Because it did so much business with railroads, Standard Oil worked out a deal with them. Standard Oil agreed to pay the same amount as other oil companies to ship its product by rail. But the railroads had a secret deal with Standard Oil. They agreed to give Standard Oil some of the money back. In fact, Standard Oil had such a sweet deal with the railroads that it got rebates, or discounts, not only on its own oil but also on oil shipped by rival companies! Because the company's shipping costs were lower, it could afford to sell oil for less than its competitors.

Extrait du]   [« *Minneapolis Times* ».

LA PIEUVRE QUI ENSERRE LE MONDE.

Le trust du pétrole, représenté ici par son chef, M. Rockefeller, enserre le monde entier dans ses puissantes tentacules, ce qui veut dire que nulle part sur le globe on ne peut échapper à sa direction pour l'extraction et la vente du pétrole.

John D. Rockefeller's control over the oil industry is illustrated in this cartoon.

Rockefeller also controlled every aspect of oil production from drilling to refining oil products. This, too, helped Standard Oil keep its prices lower than those offered by competitors.

Standard Oil managed to drive most of its competitors out of business. It sometimes bought rival companies. This meant it had fewer competitors. It used bribery and threats to keep antitrust cases against it out of court. All of these strategies allowed Rockefeller to remain "king of the oil business."

Tarbell's Reports

Ida Tarbell's reports on Standard Oil told thousands of people how the giant firm operated. Although her own father had been run out of business by Standard Oil, Tarbell tried to be evenhanded in her writing. She carefully described how the company acted, using factual sources any good reporter would use. She interviewed people who had worked at Standard Oil. She used court records and news articles in her research. Her final report contained much criticism of Standard Oil, but Tarbell rested her case on facts. The report was a great success. It was published in 1904 as a book titled, *The History of the Standard Oil Company.*

As a result of Tarbell's writings about Standard Oil, the government decided to investigate. This led to a Supreme Court ruling in 1911 breaking apart the oil trust. In the Supreme Court decision, the justice wrote, "A society in which a few men are the employers and a great body of men are merely employed or servants is not the most desirable in a republic."

After reading *McClure's* articles about Standard Oil, the public became more interested in such stories. The articles in *McClure's* were followed by work in other muckraking journals. There were articles about life insurance, fake medicine, businesses, and numerous other topics. One of these topics was the corruption of the meatpacking industry. This corruption was memorably exposed by the journalist Upton Sinclair.

Upton Sinclair

Upton Sinclair was born in Baltimore in 1878. He is best known for his book *The Jungle,* written in 1906. It is a work of fiction about the meatpacking industry.

As in the oil business, owners of certain meatpacking businesses became very wealthy toward the end of the 1800s. However, workers at meatpacking plants endured terrible, unsafe conditions for low pay.

Many people think that *The Jungle* was written to change the practices of the meatpacking industry. However, Sinclair's purpose was to raise awareness about the plight of all workers. Sinclair was a socialist—a person who believes in an economic system in which major industries are owned or regulated by the government, rather than by private businesses. As a socialist, Sinclair wrote about issues that would alert his readers to what he believed were the evils of capitalism.

Sinclair's Writings

Here is a sample of the way Sinclair tried to make these points:

> There are able-bodied men here who work from early morning until late at night, in ice-cold cellars [basements] with a quarter of an inch of water on the floor—men who for six or seven months a year never see the sunlight from Sunday afternoon till the next Sunday morning—and who cannot earn three hundred dollars in a year. There are little children here, scarce in their teens, who can hardly see the top of the work benches whose parents have lied to get them their places—and who do not make the half of three hundred dollars a year, and perhaps not even the third of it.

In passage after passage, Sinclair described the workings of the meatpacking industry. His descriptions are vivid. Some are too disgusting to read close to mealtime. He wrote about the nauseatingly unsanitary conditions in meat-processing plants. He described how pigs and cows were killed. He wrote about how the meat inspector would talk with his friends instead of inspecting the animals. Commenting on the success of his book, Sinclair said, "I aimed at the public's heart and by accident I hit it in the stomach."

After several publishers rejected *The Jungle*, Sinclair published it with his own money. Sinclair's book did more than upset people about what went into their sausages. It led President Theodore Roosevelt to order an investigation into the meatpacking business.

The workers shown here are making sausages. Upton Sinclair's revelations about the working conditions in the meatpacking industry, as well as the quality of the meat being sold to the general public, led to a federal investigation.

After *The Jungle*

The public was outraged over the details Sinclair exposed. This led the government to pass laws requiring food inspection. These laws later led to the Pure Food and Drug Act. This act allowed the government to set standards in areas such as safety and cleanliness in food processing, as well as in the advertising of food and drugs.

Today, *The Jungle* is the best known of Sinclair's books. He also wrote *King Coal*, which tells the story of a long Colorado coal strike. The book helped raise the public's awareness of union demands and poor working conditions. Sinclair later received a Pulitzer Prize for *Dragon's Teeth*, a novel about Adolf Hitler.

Sinclair did more than write to promote his socialist views. He also dreamed of building a colony of socialists in Delaware where everyone would contribute and share equally in the rewards of the work. The colony did not succeed.

Later, Sinclair moved to California, where he ran for governor. He ran as a Democrat, having decided that America was not ready to vote for a socialist. Although his election attempt failed, several of his supporters were elected to the **legislature**. Some gained control of city governments in a number of manufacturing cities.

> **Vocabulary**
> ....
> **legislature,** n. the government body responsible for making laws

Muckraking journalists made people all around the country aware of corruption in big business. Over time, the public began to appreciate the work of the muckrakers in exposing some of society's ills. This led to reforms. The meaning of the word *muckraking* then changed. Just a few years after Roosevelt first used the word, *muckraking* would be used as a badge of respect to describe the work of journalists and other reformers who uncovered sneakiness and corruption for all to see.

Chapter 3
Urban Reformers

Varieties of Reform Ida Tarbell and Upton Sinclair were not the only reformers at work during the Progressive Era. Other reformers worked hard to help the poor and improve conditions in American cities. Two of the most famous urban reformers were Jane Addams and Jacob Riis.

The Big Question

What causes did Jane Addams and Jacob Riis champion?

Jane Addams

Jane Addams was born in 1860 to a life of comfort. Her father was a man with progressive views for his time. He was against slavery. He thought that people in need should receive help. He thought that women should be educated. He helped pay for a local school so that his children could get a good education. Jane's views were shaped by her father.

For the first few years of her life she was the family favorite. But life changed for Jane when she was two years old and her mother died. When her father remarried, Jane was no longer the favorite. Jane's new stepmother had several children of her own.

Jane had conflicts with her stepmother. She wanted an education. Her stepmother was not very interested in giving Jane a good academic education. She was more interested in making Jane into a polite, socially accepted young woman. She wanted Jane to accompany her to parties. Jane wanted to finish college.

Jane Addams's childhood helped shape her work as an adult. She wanted to make a difference for those in need.

When Jane Addams's father died, she became a wealthy young woman. As many wealthy ladies did at the time, she spent two years traveling through Europe. Many young women spent their travels learning French, attending the opera, and visiting museums. Jane Addams did all of this, but a visit to London also opened her eyes to the misery of others.

Addams in Europe

In Europe, Addams witnessed a sight that had a great impact on her and haunted her for the rest of her life. In London, she saw "a myriad of hands, empty, pathetic, nerveless, and work-worn . . . clutching forward for food which was already unfit to eat." The hands belonged to poor, hungry children who were fighting over rotten vegetables.

She also observed women working in a **brewery** who were scarred from carrying tanks of burning hot beer on their backs. She challenged the owner of the brewery, who did not see anything wrong with how the employees were treated. On another trip to Europe, Addams visited what was known as a settlement. This was a community built by people who believed that in breaking down the differences among **social classes** of people, they would help poor people discover their "best selves." The settlement was staffed by young men fresh out of college. They lived in the settlement buildings and volunteered their time to help others. The people who ran the settlement offered classes to working men and their families on hundreds of topics.

> **Vocabulary**
>
> **brewery,** n. a factory that produces beer
>
> **social class,** n. a group of people who share a similar way of life and level of importance or influence in society

Addams interviewed many people at the settlement. In her view, it succeeded because the place had a homey feeling. Almost instantly, Jane Addams knew what she wanted to do for the rest of her life—to create a community like this, to improve the lives of poor families like those she had met. She would create a settlement in Chicago, devoted to the needs of immigrant families, and the settlement would be staffed by educated young women.

Jane Addams saw a great deal of poverty on the streets of London. There men, women, and children begged for food.

Hull House

Jane Addams searched Chicago for the perfect spot to fulfill her dream. When she found it, she called it Hull House. At first, Hull House was surrounded by mud and filth, in a neighborhood where children chased rats for fun.

About the neighborhood where Hull House was built, Addams wrote, "The streets were inexpressibly dirty, the number of schools inadequate, factory **legislation** unenforced, the street-lighting bad, the paving miserable."

These were the neighborhoods where Chicago's immigrants lived. At the time, many native-born Americans did not welcome immigrants, but Addams believed that the culture of the United States would be made richer by contact with the cultures brought by these people from Italy, Germany, Poland, Russia, and Czechoslovakia.

Jane convinced several wealthy people to provide money to renovate the run-down building. She also spent thousands of dollars of her own money to fix up Hull House, which she opened in 1889.

Addams labeled Hull House a settlement. In her view, it would become a loving, trusting community where education was the most important thing. On the morning the settlement opened, local children threw rocks at the building, breaking one of the newly washed windows. But Addams refused to give up hope. Within days, dozens of neighbors came calling— washerwomen, peddlers, factory workers, and many more. The house became a magnet for children as well.

Hull House had bathtubs for those people in the neighborhood who had no plumbing. It had kitchens where good nutrition was taught. It had a day-care center. Each day of the week a different group of immigrants was invited to come share their traditions—songs, ideas, holidays, customs—with younger generations.

Jane Addams founded Hull House to help immigrant families settle in Chicago. Here you can see the cover of a book written about Hull House.

But not everyone approved of the settlement. One neighborhood policeman said to Jane Addams, "Lady, you oughtn't to let bums like these come here."

More Settlement Houses

Jane Addams had many supporters, though, and she spread the word about her successes at Hull House. Soon, Addams's ideas spread around the country. By the end of the 1890s, settlement houses modeled after Hull House had been built in several large cities. The settlement houses had gymnasiums where people living in crowded conditions could get exercise. Language classes taught people to speak English so they could communicate with their new neighbors. For thousands of immigrant families, these settlement houses eased the pains associated with moving to a new country and adjusting to a foreign culture.

Jane Addams's efforts in the reform movement were not limited to Hull House. Later in life she joined the political movement aimed at getting women the right to vote. She believed that if women were going to bring about big changes in society, they needed to be able to vote. Jane Addams became friends with Theodore Roosevelt, who visited Hull House several times. She seconded the nomination of Theodore Roosevelt for the office of president. She was the first woman to do such a thing. She was also active in the formation of the NAACP, the National Association for the Advancement of Colored People.

> **Vocabulary**
>
> "second the nomination," (phrase) agree with the proposal to appoint or elect a person for something

When World War I broke out, Jane Addams spoke out against the war. She was elected head of the Women's Peace Party, whose mission was a "women's war against war." These actions made her unpopular with people who thought patriots should support the war. Addams was labeled a communist, which was a way of calling her un-American or unpatriotic. Still, Jane Addams's long years of work in social reform did not go unnoticed. In 1931, she received the Nobel Peace Prize for her life's work.

Theodore Roosevelt and Jane Addams were friends. Both championed similar causes. Theodore believed that women should be allowed to vote.

Jacob Riis

Jane Addams was the great champion of the poor people of Chicago. Jacob Riis (/rees/) was the great champion of the poor people of New York City. Riis was a Danish carpenter. He arrived in the United States in 1870, when he was twenty years old. At the time, the United States was going through a **depression**. The young immigrant was unable to find a job. He ate handouts from Delmonico's, a fancy restaurant in New York. When he had a nickel, he would spend it to have a bed in a men's rooming house.

One of the worst nights Riis spent was in a police station where homeless men were allowed to sleep. His most prized possession, a necklace, was stolen. His beloved dog, Bob, was killed. Riis decided he would do all he could to end the abuses that were so common in these shelters.

> **Vocabulary**
>
> **depression,** n. an extended period of reduced economic activity, when large numbers of people cannot find jobs and most people have less money to spend

Riis Becomes a Reporter

His rough-and-tumble experiences led Riis to decide he must tell the world about the sufferings of the poor immigrants. He was determined to become a reporter.

Riis later explained, "It seemed to me that a reporter's was the highest and noblest of all callings; no one could sift right from wrong as he, and punish the wrong."

Riis went from one newspaper to another, seeking work. Rejected by one editor who laughed as Riis explained that he had experience as a carpenter, Riis replied, "You laugh! You laugh now, but wait—." By the end of his career, Riis would be the one to laugh. He would show the world the good that a muckraking reporter could accomplish. Not long after, Riis did gain some experience as a reporter, and he set out on a campaign of reform.

Night after night, Riis roamed New York to uncover the city's dirty secrets. Throughout Riis's time as a reporter, he used basic detective work to follow story leads. Often, Riis persisted even when other reporters made fun of him or tried to show that his conclusions were wrong.

Once, in the middle of a **cholera epidemic**, Riis traced the New York City water supply north into the countryside. He discovered that the streams that led to the drinking water supply were contaminated. People bathed and washed their dogs in the streams. Town dumps sat right on the banks of the rivers. His competitors insisted that Riis was wrong. They said the cholera germs would never live the length of time needed for the water to travel into the New York City drinking supply. Riis found that it took four days for a drop of cholera-infected water to complete its journey. The virus lived for seven days. Riis's theory was right.

> ## Vocabulary
>
> "cholera epidemic," (phrase) a situation in which cholera, a serious bacterial infection of the intestine, spreads to many people in an area or region

Jacob Riis worked to improve the lives of poor families.

How the Other Half Lives

Later, a twist of fate led Riis to get a job reporting on the same part of
New York where he had once been homeless. One of his goals was to rid
the city of its dirty, unsafe tenement buildings. Many immigrant families

lived crowded into these buildings. Riis described the ghastly conditions in a typical New York tenement:

> The hall is dark and you might stumble over the children pitching pennies back there. Not that it would hurt them; kicks and cuffs [slaps] are their daily diet. They have little else. Here where the hall turns and dives into utter darkness is a step, and another, another. A flight of stairs. You can feel your way, if you cannot see it. Close . . . [stuffy; without air]. Yes! What would you have? All the fresh air that ever enters these stairs comes from the hall-door that is forever slamming, and from the windows of dark bedrooms that in turn receive from the stairs their sole supply of the elements [such as wind and rain] God meant to be free, but man deals out with such [a miserly] hand. That was a woman filling her pail [bucket] by the hydrant you just bumped against. The sinks are in the hallway, that all the tenants may have access and all be poisoned alike by their summer stenches [bad smells].
>
> . . . Here is a door. Listen! That short hacking cough, that tiny, helpless wail—what do they mean? They mean that the soiled bow of white [baby] you saw on the door downstairs will have another story to tell— Oh! a sadly familiar story—before the day is at an end. The child is dying with measles. With half a chance it might have lived; but it had none. That dark bedroom killed it.

That is how Riis described the experience of immigrants living in New York tenement buildings in his book, *How the Other Half Lives*. No fresh air, no sunlight, poor health, and even poorer **sanitation**. Not a pretty sight, is it?

At first, Riis's writing did not reach many readers. He said, "I wrote, but it seemed to make no impression." Soon Riis discovered a new tool that would help him drive home his message—a flashbulb that could be used with a camera to take pictures in the dark. Riis learned how to take pictures and develop them himself. Armed with a camera, he went into the darkest corners of tenements to record the depths of human misery.

The pictures of hopelessness lent a face to Riis's written descriptions of the tenements. Often, the photos were used as evidence when landlords tried to dispute claims that Riis made to the Board of Health.

As Riis began to give lectures on his findings, he showed his audiences "magic lantern" pictures. These early slide shows helped drive home the points Riis made about the horror of the tenements.

Jacob Riis was a powerful writer and photographer who exposed the poor living conditions of immigrants in New York City. This photograph was taken by Jacob Riis in 1890. It shows a place known as Bandit's Roost on Mulberry Street in New York City's lower Manhattan area. It was crime ridden and dangerous with a great deal of poverty.

More Revelations

Riis's muckraking covered many topics. He described his work as a reporter like this: "It is all a great human drama in which these things are the acts that mean grief, suffering, revenge upon somebody, loss or gain."

Riis wrote about children who did not go to school. He was also concerned about children who spent their days cooped up in dark, windowless rooms. Sunshine, Riis insisted, "is a child's right, and [the child] is not to be cheated of it."

Riis recognized that, without a safe place to play, some children resorted to vandalism. He fought with the Board of Education to turn schools into neighborhood centers so that children would have a place for clubs and recreation at night.

Another area of reform for Riis involved the use of underage children as workers in factories. He kept a chart on his desk showing the ages at which

The image shows two young girls who were employed to work in a clothing factory.

children developed their different teeth. He used this chart to prove to the factory owners that many of the factory workers who claimed to be fourteen or fifteen were actually much younger than that.

"All things come to those who wait—and fight for them," Riis had declared. So it was with enormous pride that he ignored the "Keep off the Grass" sign at Mulberry Park in New York City. After years of work, Riis had succeeded in having several blocks of tenements purchased and torn down by the city. In their place, was a grass-filled park where children could play.

After Riis's success in cleaning up the tenements, Theodore Roosevelt described the reporter as "the most useful citizen in America." In the introduction to Riis's autobiography, *The Making of an American*, Roosevelt wrote:

> Riis was one of those men who by his writings contributed most to the standard of unselfishness, of disinterestedness, of sane and kindly good citizenship. . . . He was one of the few real writers for clean and decent living who was also a great doer. He never wrote sentences which he did not in good faith try to act whenever he could find the opportunity for action.

Chapter 4
Theodore Roosevelt

Rough Riding Reformer One of America's greatest reformers was Theodore Roosevelt. Theodore Roosevelt was a Harvard graduate, a cowboy, a world traveler, a Nobel Prize winner, a soldier, an admirer of Jane Addams and Jacob Riis, and the twenty-sixth president of the United States.

The Big Question

Why might it be true to say that Theodore Roosevelt was a champion of the American people?

A Boy with Determination

The future president was born into a well-known, socially prominent family in 1858. As a child, Theodore (Teddy) Roosevelt was small and sickly, and suffered from asthma. He was so nearsighted that when some friends were reading a message on a billboard one day, he realized, "Not only was I unable to read the sign but I could not even see the letters." Soon he got a pair of eyeglasses and was very excited. "I had no idea how beautiful the world was until I got those spectacles," he later wrote.

When Roosevelt was a boy, his father told him that, with his poor health and feeble body, he wouldn't amount to much. The boy replied with determination, "I'll *make* my body."

Roosevelt enjoyed nature. He loved to spend time in the country collecting specimens of plants and animals. He created his own Roosevelt Museum of Natural History at the age of eight.

Teddy Roosevelt became so active that once, as president, he asked a visiting ambassador what he would like to do after they had spent a day exercising with a medicine ball, running, and playing tennis. The ambassador replied, "If it's all the same to you, Mr. President, I'd like to lie [down] and die."

A Start in Politics

Roosevelt attended Harvard University. From Harvard, Roosevelt decided to go into politics, serving in the New York State legislature. After his wife and mother both died on the same day, Roosevelt went west to distract himself from his losses.

On his return east two years later, Roosevelt threw himself back into politics. He headed the New York Civil Service Commission, a government organization that helped make sure that only qualified people got government jobs. In the past, these jobs had been handed out by political bosses in exchange for votes, bribes, and other favors. Roosevelt also served as president of the Board of Police Commissioners in New York City. He liked to get directly involved by working with people like Jacob Riis.

While Roosevelt was police commissioner in New York, Jacob Riis asked him whether he was thinking about running for president in an upcoming election. Roosevelt was upset by the question.

"Don't you ever put such ideas in my head," he told Riis. "No friend of mine would ever say a thing like that. Never, ever, must . . . you remind a man on a political job that he may be president. It almost always kills him politically. He loses his nerve; he can't do his work; he gives up the very traits [characteristics] that are making him a possibility."

As if thinking out loud, Roosevelt also said, "I must be wanting to be president. Every young man does. But I won't let myself think of it; I must not because if I do, I will begin to work for it, I'll be careful, calculating, cautious in word and act, and so—I'll beat myself. See?"

The Rough Riders (seen here) were a voluntary cavalry that fought in the Spanish-American War. The war began when Cuba fought for independence from Spain in 1895. The war extended into the Americas and the Philippines. Colonel Roosevelt, seen in the center of the image, was the leader of the Rough Riders.

Perhaps Roosevelt put the thought of becoming president out of his mind. Or perhaps he continued to think about it as he went off to fight in Cuba during the Spanish-American War.

When he returned in 1898, Roosevelt was hailed as a hero for his adventures in Cuba with a regiment called the Rough Riders. The war hero was quickly elected governor of New York. It was then that Roosevelt began to build on his reputation as a fighter for the public good.

From Governor to White House

In earlier chapters you learned about trusts—the large, powerful organizations that controlled certain industries. You also learned about some laws that were intended to control these trusts. When Theodore Roosevelt became governor of New York State, he soon realized that existing antitrust laws were not effective. They did not work. The Sherman Antitrust Act, passed under President Harrison in 1890, was one such law. Instead of controlling businesses, the act had been used to stop union actions.

Because of his interest in reforming government and replacing trusts, Roosevelt was not popular with many legislators in his own party, who liked things just the way they were. They called him a *goo-goo*. This name was given to reformers who wanted good government. Party bosses wanted to find a way to get Roosevelt out of New York politics.

In 1900, President McKinley was running for a second term against William Jennings Bryan, whom he had defeated four years earlier. As the reform movement became more popular, McKinley decided that he should have a reform-minded **running mate** such as Roosevelt.

At the time, some of Roosevelt's opponents in New York were trying to silence him on the issue

Vocabulary

running mate, n. a political partner also running for office

When President William McKinley ran for reelection in 1900, he chose Theodore Roosevelt as his running mate.

of trusts. They thought the best way to get him out of the way—and out of New York—would be to make him vice president. This office was considered a dead end in politics. Roosevelt knew it; he told a friend he knew he would "simply be shelved as vice president."

In loyalty to the Republican Party, however, Roosevelt reluctantly accepted the nomination as vice president. McKinley and Roosevelt were elected in 1900, defeating the great public speaker William Jennings Bryan. Less than a year later, Roosevelt's career took a sudden turn when McKinley was assassinated, and Roosevelt became president.

At first, Roosevelt continued McKinley's Republican policies, largely favoring big business. But not long after Roosevelt took office, he had a chance to prove himself as a reformer.

A Strong and Determined President

In 1902, Roosevelt faced an energy shortage. Coal miners in Pennsylvania went on strike. They were seeking higher wages and better working conditions. Soon, schools and hospitals that relied on coal were running out of fuel.

For a time, union leaders and mine owners refused even to discuss a solution. Roosevelt decided it was time for him to step in. He wanted to make the union leaders and mine owners settle their disagreements. He threatened to use federal troops to take over the mines if the union leaders and mine owners did not come up with a solution. In this way, the strike was ended.

Roosevelt was determined to take on the trusts on a national level. As he wrote in his autobiography, "It was imperative to teach the masters of the biggest corporations in the land that they were not, and would not be permitted to regard themselves as, above the law."

Not long into his first term as president, Roosevelt became concerned with the railroads. A company owned by J.P. Morgan had control of three railroads. Roosevelt thought this was a violation of the Sherman Antitrust Act. Before this, the act had been used by the government to break up union strikes.

The cartoon shows the owners and controllers of the trusts, the wealthy and powerful businessmen, being weakened and made poor by Theodore Roosevelt.

It had not been used to oppose the powerful trusts. Roosevelt decided to test the antitrust act by taking Morgan's Northern Securities Company to court.

When Morgan heard of the president's plan, he asked, "Are you going to attack my other interests, the Steel Trust and the others?"

Roosevelt responded, "Certainly not, unless we find out that in any case they have done something that we regard as wrong."

Even before the case was settled, Roosevelt took on other trusts. Then in 1903, Roosevelt was able to sign into law three antitrust measures, including the Elkins Act, which did away with the railroad rebates you read about earlier.

Roosevelt's Second Term

In 1904, Roosevelt decided to seek another term in office. This time, he would take office by popular vote, not by an assassin's bullet. The idea of a "square deal" became the theme for Roosevelt's new campaign. He hoped that all Americans would get fair treatment and a chance for a good life. He called this a "square deal." This idea made Roosevelt very popular, and he won the 1904 election by a wide margin. The ordinary people of the United States had spoken in favor of reform.

During his next four years as president, Roosevelt continued to press for controls on big business. The railroads were his first target. Under Roosevelt's administration, the Interstate Commerce Commission gained more power than it had earlier. The commission supposedly could control commerce between the states, but it had not been a strong **regulatory body** until Roosevelt backed its actions. Under Roosevelt, the commission got the authority to control railroad shipping rates.

Teddy Bears

Did you ever wonder where teddy bears got their name? The name comes from President Theodore Roosevelt. Teddy, as the popular leader was also called, loved nature and hunting. In 1902, the president traveled to Mississippi to go bear hunting. He discovered a lonely cub someone had tied to a tree. Roosevelt was a famed hunter. But he was unwilling to shoot the captive cub. A newspaper cartoonist illustrated the story for the world to see. Soon stuffed toy bears—"teddy" bears, named for the president— became very popular.

A cartoon helped spread the story of Roosevelt's refusal to shoot a captive bear cub.

Roosevelt pushed for reform in other areas as well. Following the uproar over Upton Sinclair's *The Jungle*, Roosevelt signed the Pure Food and Drug Act in 1906. Roosevelt also worked to break apart John Rockefeller's Standard Oil.

It's important to understand, however, that Roosevelt was not anti-business. He simply wanted to make sure that there were fair practices in place so that owners of small businesses, as well as ordinary workers, were given a fair chance to succeed and to improve their lives.

Saving National Resources

Theodore Roosevelt was a champion of captive bear cubs and the great outdoors. He went on to make an important contribution to saving the nation's **natural resources**. After the Civil War, railroad and timber companies acquired huge areas of lands, particularly in the West. They had

> **Vocabulary**
>
> **natural resource,** n. something from nature that is useful to humans

no interest in preserving the natural resources, such as forests, minerals, lakes, and rivers, found on these lands. Their main interest was to use these resources to make as much money as possible.

Roosevelt, in contrast, had a great understanding and appreciation of all natural resources, especially forests. Here is how Roosevelt explained the need to preserve forests:

> A primeval [very old] forest is a great sponge which absorbs and distills [cleans] the rainwater. And when it is destroyed the result is apt to be an alternation of flood and drought. Forest fires ultimately make the land a desert. . . . Every effort should be made to minimize their destructive influence. We need to have our system of forestry gradually developed and conducted along scientific principles. When this has been done it will be possible to allow marketable lumber [wood] to be cut everywhere without damage to the forests. . . . But until lumbering [the cutting down

Stanislaus National Forest in California (seen here) is one of the oldest national forests in America.

of trees] is thus conducted, on strictly scientific principles no less than upon principles of the strictest honesty toward the State, we cannot afford to suffer it at all in the State forests. Unrestrained greed means the ruin of the great woods and the drying up of the sources of the rivers.

Under Roosevelt's administration, the Forestry Division of the federal Land Office became responsible for the wise use of the nation's forest lands—those that were not already in private hands. The government's approach centered on the prevention of forest fires and on controlling lumbering, grazing, and mining on government-owned lands. During Roosevelt's terms as president, the amount of national forest grew from 47 million acres to 195 million acres—much of which was bought back from private owners.

National Parks

Decades before Roosevelt's time, the federal government granted the state of California the right to use the Yosemite Valley and surrounding area as a park for public recreation and enjoyment. Yosemite is a beautiful area. It is filled with forests, majestic waterfalls, rock formations, and wide meadows. In 1890, Yosemite was made a national park. But California retained control of Yosemite Valley, where some of the most famous rock formations, forests, and meadows are. When Roosevelt visited the region in 1903 with **naturalist** John Muir, he was outraged to see how the park was being abused. Huge numbers of trees had been cut down, and sheep grazed wherever they pleased.

President Roosevelt was one of our nation's first **conservationists**. Here he visits Yosemite Valley, in California, with John Muir.

Roosevelt thought there was nothing more beautiful than the region's groves of giant redwood trees. He believed that "the people should see to it that they are reserved for their children and their children's children."

In 1906, all of Yosemite finally came under federal control, and one of the nation's greatest natural wonders was saved for future generations to enjoy.

Congress did not support the president in many of his conservation efforts. However, the **Antiquities** Act of 1906 allowed the president to name certain places as national **landmarks**. Without the agreement of Congress, he could set aside buildings and places of natural or historic interest to be protected from development.

Vocabulary
....

naturalist, n. an expert in natural history; a person who studies nature

conservationist, n. a person who wants to stop human actions that are harmful to wild or natural spaces

antiquities, n. objects from ancient times

landmark, n. an area or a structure that has special significance

Roosevelt decided to declare certain special places national landmarks to help keep the areas safe from destruction. Under the Antiquities Act, Roosevelt was able to set aside eighteen different areas that Congress refused to make national parks. These included Devil's Tower in Wyoming, and the Petrified Forest and Grand Canyon in Arizona.

For Roosevelt, another important area of conservation was the preservation of wildlife. At that time, many species of birds and animals were threatened with extinction. During buffalo hunts, hunters shot at buffalo from inside trains. The popularity of these hunts led to a sharp decrease in buffalo populations. Bird populations were also on the decline. Millions and millions of birds had been killed for their decorative feathers.

Roosevelt had loved birds since childhood. On a visit to Florida's Pelican Island in 1903, he asked, "Is there any law that prevents me declaring Pelican Island a National Bird Sanctuary?" He answered his question before anyone could interfere. "Very well, then, I do declare it." During his term as president, Roosevelt created fifty such animal refuges, or safe places.

But Roosevelt's conservation efforts caused him trouble, especially in the West, where abuse of natural resources was at its peak. Many of his acts made him unpopular with loggers and miners who depended on these resources to make a living.

Roosevelt made Pelican Island a protected bird sanctuary in 1903.

Stepping Down

Roosevelt had promised that he would not run again when his second term was up in 1909. He was true to his word. He left the presidency at the end of his term in March 1909, and traveled to Africa for a long hunting trip.

Theodore Roosevelt realized that Taft was unable to continue the work that he had begun.

Roosevelt's hand-picked successor, William Howard Taft, was elected. At first he continued many of the trust-busting efforts begun by Roosevelt. But Taft had little political experience, and soon the Progressive movement was losing ground in Congress as President Taft's policies were rejected. Progressives began to feel betrayed by Taft.

In 1912, Roosevelt decided to run again for the presidency. He wanted to fight again for reform. It was in this political race that Jane Addams supported him and nominated him. Because Taft had the support of the regular Republican Party, Roosevelt now ran as the candidate for the Progressive, or Bull Moose, Party. This unusual name was applied to the Progressive Party when, in response to a reporter's question about his health, Roosevelt replied that he felt "as strong as a bull moose."

The clash between Taft and Roosevelt—basically two Republicans—split the vote of reform-minded Republicans. Socialist reformer Eugene Debs was also in the running, but the Democratic candidate, Woodrow Wilson, also a reform candidate, won the election. Defeated, Roosevelt finally retired from politics.

Roosevelt never lost his love of exploring nature and the wilderness. His travels took him around the world. After his last term as president, Roosevelt journeyed down the Amazon River, where he fell ill with a fever that destroyed his health. Despite this, he said, "I had to go. It was my last chance to be a boy."

Theodore Roosevelt championed many causes that made life better for ordinary Americans.

Chapter 5
Reform for African Americans

Freedom and Struggle After the Civil War, a series of changes were made to the U.S. Constitution. These new amendments began a revolution in the position of African Americans in our country.

The Big Question

What were the Jim Crow laws, and what were the views of Ida B. Wells, Booker T. Washington, and W.E.B. Du Bois in terms of gaining rights for African Americans?

The Thirteenth Amendment to the Constitution was ratified in December 1865. It officially ended slavery in America. The Fourteenth Amendment was ratified in 1868. It made all former enslaved people citizens of the United States. It also guaranteed them equal protection under the law and certain voting rights. Finally, the Fifteenth Amendment was ratified in 1870. This amendment stated that the right to vote "shall not be denied or abridged [limited] by the United States or any state on account of race, color, or previous condition of servitude [slavery]." These amendments changed the rules in a society in which one race had long dominated another.

However, following the Civil War, there were still years of turmoil. White Americans made unfair laws called Jim Crow laws. These state laws were made in many parts of the country, including Southern and Midwestern states. They were

Jim Crow laws kept Americans apart from each other.

designed to keep African Americans from really having the rights granted by the Thirteenth, Fourteenth, and Fifteenth amendments.

Jim Crow laws kept African Americans and white people separated from each other in many ways. It was against the law in certain places for African Americans and white people to ride in the same train car, to sit in the same waiting room at a bus station, to play a game of checkers with each other, to swear on the same Bible in court, to use the same water fountain or public bathroom, or to bury their dogs in the same cemetery.

Segregation

In 1896, the U.S. Supreme Court determined that these "separate but equal" laws that **segregated** people by race were not illegal. It wasn't until 1954 that another Supreme Court decision overruled the 1896 decision.

The Jim Crow laws tried to keep people separate. Probably more important were laws that kept African Americans from voting. These laws stopped African Americans from exercising their political rights and power.

For many years, laws ensured that African Americans were not only separated from white people, but also that African Americans did not have equal rights. Several reformers devoted their lives to bringing about equal rights and opportunities for all African Americans. Among these reformers were Ida B. Wells, Booker T. Washington, and W E. B. Du Bois.

These three **civil rights** leaders did not always agree on what methods should be followed to ensure equal civil rights for African Americans. Often, Du Bois and Wells criticized Washington for his approach to improving the lives of African Americans. Yet they all agreed that these efforts would be the focus of their work.

> **Vocabulary**
>
> **segregate,** v.
> to keep people separate, usually on the basis of race
>
> **civil rights,** n.
> certain rights, such as the right to vote, or the right to a fair trial, that are guaranteed by the Constitution and its amendments to all American citizens

Ida B. Wells

Ida Bell Wells was an African American born into slavery in 1862. Her grandparents were a white plantation owner and an enslaved woman. She was considered an African American and was enslaved. When she was just a toddler, the Civil War ended. She and her family were freed.

Ida B. Wells

Ida Wells's parents understood the value of education and hard work. After receiving their freedom, they worked to purchase their own home and save money. Wells attended Rust College. But she was dismissed for a disagreement with the president of the institution. She later regretted that her bad temper had cut short her education.

A few months later, Wells's parents died. After that, she took care of the household and the other children in her family. During this time, she was criticized by her neighbors. They felt that it wasn't proper for a young lady to live without a parent or guardian. Once her grandmother moved in to help, Wells was able to find a teaching position in Memphis to help support the children.

Living apart from her family and commuting home on weekends, Ida Wells spent much of her time reading. The books she read filled her head with a desire to do something heroic and with a distaste for weak, silly heroines.

A Sense of Fairness

The Jim Crow laws said that Ida Wells had to sit in a different train car from that of white passengers. Trains in the South in the late 1800s had "ladies' cars" where smoking and swearing were not permitted. African American women were not permitted to sit in these cars. Yet women who did not sit in the ladies' cars were looked down upon as being unladylike.

One weekend, Ida Wells purchased a first-class ticket entitling her to sit in the ladies' car on the train home from Memphis. The conductor told her to move to the smoking car. Wells refused. When the conductor tried to force her out of her seat, she bit him. Later, Wells sued the railroad. Other African American women had also sued over similar treatment.

For several years, on and off, Wells tried to fight being ejected from the ladies' car. She had mixed success in the courts. Finally, Wells found a way to express her outrage over injustice. She began writing for a local newspaper owned by African American ministers. Her experience with the courts was the topic of her first article.

Anti-lynching Campaign

In 1892, competition in the grocery business in Memphis led to an attack on the African American owners of a grocery store. Several African American men were arrested. One night, three of them were kidnapped from jail. They were taken out into the countryside and shot. One of the men was a close friend of Ida Wells.

Memphis was not the only place where murders as well as **lynchings** took place. Mob attacks on African Americans had occurred for years, but now they were increasing. Mobs accused African Americans of crimes, then killed them, claiming they deserved this punishment. Wells wrote about these injustices in newspaper editorials. Her writing prompted violence against the newspaper and threats against her.

Wells urged a **boycott** of Memphis streetcars and white-owned businesses to protest the lynchings.

Vocabulary

lynching, n. the killing of a person by a mob, often by hanging

boycott, n. a form of organized protest in which people refuse to buy goods or have anything to do with a particular group or country

She even urged African Americans who could afford to leave Memphis to do so. Taking Wells's advice, many African Americans moved to Northern cities. Wells herself was fearful of remaining in the South. She left to work for a Northern newspaper.

Lynchings continued throughout the country for many years, most notably in the South. In the 1890s, hundreds of African American men and women were killed. Wells was shocked and angered by these lynchings. She wrote many articles expressing her outrage. Eventually Wells found some support for her anti-lynching position in Northern newspapers. She traveled widely to speak on the issue of lynching. For many years she wrote and lectured on this topic. She published a book called *A Red Record* that cataloged lynchings in the United States. In it, she wrote: "We demand a fair trial by law for those accused of crime, and punishment by law after honest conviction. . . . Surely the **humanitarian** spirit of this country . . . will no longer refuse to lift its voice on this subject."

> ## Vocabulary
>
> **humanitarian,** adj. caring about the well-being of all people

Wells tried again and again to shame Americans into taking action against lynch mobs. She wrote:

> Nowhere in the civilized world save the United States of America do men, possessing all civil and political power, go out in bands of 50 and 5,000 to hunt down, shoot, hang or burn to death a single individual, unarmed and absolutely powerless. Statistics show that nearly 10,000 American citizens have been lynched in the past 20 years. . . . We refuse to believe this country, so powerful to defend its citizens abroad, is unable to protect its citizens at home.

Much of Wells's writing and speaking was devoted to the topic of lynching. But she also worked frequently with other black leaders, including Booker T. Washington and W.E.B. Du Bois, to secure better treatment of African Americans and to organize their political power.

Booker T. Washington   W.E.B. Du Bois

Wells died in 1931, without seeing a federal anti-lynching bill passed. But her efforts drew attention to this terrible phenomenon and advanced the budding civil rights movement.

Booker T. Washington

Like Ida Wells, Booker T. Washington was born enslaved and was freed after the Civil War.

Education became a driving force in the life of Booker T. Washington. While he was enslaved, one of his chores was to carry the schoolbooks of the plantation owner's daughter when she went to school and came home. Peeking into the schoolroom gave the young boy "the feeling that to get into a school house and study in this way would be about the same as getting into paradise."

After the Civil War, Washington's family moved to West Virginia. There, at home, Washington taught himself the alphabet. A school opened for African Americans near Washington's home. But his stepfather would not allow

Booker T. Washington was born in this tiny house in western Virginia. He was nine years old when the Civil War ended.

Booker to go to the school. Instead, he had to work in a salt mine to earn money to support the family. Booker begged to go to school. His pleading eventually led to an agreement. His stepfather agreed that Booker could attend school if he worked before and after school. The young boy worked for several hours until nine in the morning. He then worked again after school for several more hours.

Washington still had one problem. School began at nine o'clock in the morning. He had to walk several miles to get from the mine to the school. Washington solved the problem by sneaking into the mine office and changing the clock from eight-thirty to nine. This gave him a half hour to walk and not be late for school.

Further Education

After the Civil War, many former enslaved people of all ages wanted to receive an education, Washington was determined to continue his. In 1872, he enrolled at the Hampton Normal and Agricultural Institute in Virginia. To pay for his room and board at school, Washington took a job as a janitor at the institute. After he graduated in 1875, he took two jobs. During the daytime, he worked as a teacher of African American children. In the evenings, he taught African American adults.

He also continued his own education at Wayland Seminary in Washington, D.C. After finishing his studies at the seminary, he went back to teach at the Hampton Institute.

Washington began to believe that people who learned a trade in school, such as being a blacksmith or a tinsmith, were better prepared for a life of freedom than people who learned only traditional school subjects, such as reading, writing, and arithmetic.

Washington had great respect for people who worked with their hands. He admired people who had a skill and could transform that skill into economic security by working at good jobs. Washington believed that political power flowed from economic power. He wanted to build the economic power of African Americans as a first step toward building political power. The first step in building that economic power was, Washington believed, learning how to do a job or practice a trade well.

Washington became the founder and first principal of the Tuskegee Normal and Industrial Institute, a school for African American adults. Tuskegee Institute later became Tuskegee University.

In addition to formal studies or "book learning," as Washington called typical schoolwork, Washington decided that every Tuskegee student would learn a trade. The students at the new school would begin by actually building the buildings where they would study. The students built fifty-one of the school's sixty buildings. They used bricks they made by hand. They became very successful at making and selling the bricks. In one year, they made more than a million bricks for use at the institute and for sale to the community.

In this photograph, taken in 1906, you can see students standing at the entrance to the Tuskegee Institute in Alabama. The gates were called the Lincoln Gates.

"Our knowledge must be harnessed to the stuff of real things," Washington said. He believed that the key to success for former enslaved people was to learn skills that would allow them to help build and profit from a new South.

As Tuskegee Institute grew and succeeded, so did Booker T. Washington's reputation. He was invited to give speeches about the institute's success. One of the most important addresses he gave was at the Atlanta Exposition of 1895, where the work of Tuskegee students was on display.

Students attending the Tuskegee Institute helped build the school.

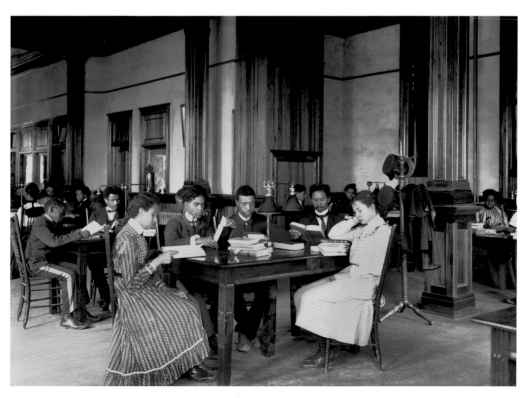

In this photograph, you can see students studying in the library at the Tuskegee Institute.

Atlanta Exposition Address

The 1895 Atlanta Exposition was a big public event.
Washington was an important African American
leader. He was invited to address the huge crowd
at the Atlanta Exposition. On September 18, 1895,
Washington suggested a **compromise** in the
relationship between African Americans and white
people. He urged African Americans to avoid
strikes and unions in their quest for fairness. He asked for an acceptance of
Jim Crow laws that were in existence. Washington declared that the struggle
for "social equality is the extremest folly." Above all, he called for patience.
He suggested that African Americans should be content to be separate
from white people.

In his speech, Washington compared the situation of African Americans in
the late 1800s to people on a ship lost at sea. The people on the ship are in
desperate need of water. They think they can obtain fresh water only from
another ship. But they eventually find their drinking water in a place where
they had never thought to look:

> A ship lost at sea for many days suddenly sighted a friendly vessel. From
> the mast of the unfortunate vessel was seen a signal, "Water, water; we
> die of thirst." The answer from the friendly vessel came back, "Cast down
> your bucket where you are." A second time the signal, "Water, water;
> send us water!" ran up from the distressed vessel, and was answered,
> "Cast down your bucket where you are."

> The captain of the distressed vessel, at last heeded the injunction
> [instruction] to cast down his bucket and it came up full of fresh,
> sparkling water from the mouth of the Amazon River.

> To those of my race who depend on bettering their condition in a
> foreign land or who underestimate the importance of cultivating friendly

relations with the Southern white man, who is their next-door neighbor, I would say "Cast down your bucket where you are"—cast it down in making friends in the manly way of the people of all races by whom we are surrounded.

Washington used the image of the ship to encourage African Americans to stay where they were and make use of the resources around them. He thought they should not move away from the South or leave the United States. Instead, Washington thought African Americans should develop their own resources and abilities. He wanted them to cultivate good relations with the white people in the areas where they lived.

Many in the audience rushed to congratulate Washington on his address. A Southern newspaper editor sent a telegraph to New York with this message: "I do not exaggerate when I say that Professor Booker T. Washington's address

This photograph was taken during the celebrations of the Tuskegee's twenty-fifth anniversary. Standing with Booker T. Washington are (left to right), Robert C. Ogden, Senator William Howard Taft, and Andrew Carnegie.

yesterday was one of the most notable speeches, both as to character and as to the warmth of his reception, ever delivered to a Southern audience." Another paper referred to him as the "Negro Moses." President Grover Cleveland sent a letter of praise and called on Washington for advice on matters relating to African Americans.

Washington had a powerful impact on his audiences, both white and black. In his diary, Washington wrote that many white people would come up to him after a speech to shake his hand. Many of them would comment that this was "the first time they had ever called a Negro 'Mister.'"

Washington's message of patience and compromise was not nearly as well received by other African American leaders. Many disagreed with his approach to gaining civil rights and living in a society governed by white people. In time, Ida B. Wells came to oppose many of Washington's views, and one of his most outspoken critics was W E. B. Du Bois.

W. E. B. Du Bois

William Edward Burghardt (W.E.B.) Du Bois (/doo*boyz/) strongly opposed Booker T. Washington's ideas. Du Bois said that Washington wanted African Americans to give up three things that were essential to progress: political power, civil rights, and higher education. Du Bois insisted that the effect of this would be for African Americans to become second-class citizens.

In contrast to Washington, Du Bois felt that the "color line"—the invisible barrier that segregated African Americans and white people in all areas of life—must be broken. Indeed, he singled out the color line as the crucial problem of the age:

> The problem of the twentieth century is the problem of the color line— the relation of the darker to the lighter races of men in Asia and Africa, in America and the islands of the sea. It was a phase of this problem that caused the Civil War; . . . we know, that the question of Negro slavery was the real cause of the conflict. Curious it was, too, how this deeper question ever forced itself to the surface despite effort and disclaimer [denial].

Early Years

The different opinions that Du Bois and Washington had might have come from their different backgrounds.

In 1868, Du Bois was born in the North. Washington was born on a Southern plantation. Whereas Washington was self-educated, Du Bois was educated at good schools. He was a star pupil. He was one of only two African American students in his high school class.

After high school, Du Bois received a scholarship to Fisk University in Nashville, Tennessee. Later, he became the first African American to receive a Ph.D. degree from Harvard.

After Harvard, Du Bois traveled and taught widely. He conducted research into the lives of African Americans. He concluded that freeing those who were enslaved had made Southern white people even more prejudiced than before.

Du Bois rejected Booker T. Washington's call for compromise. In his book *The Souls of Black Folk*, Du Bois was highly critical of Washington. Du Bois

W.E.B. Du Bois received his Ph.D. from Harvard in 1895.

believed that the ideas in Washington's Atlanta speech would cause African Americans to lose their civil rights for the sake of better economic opportunity.

Du Bois wrote:

> So far as Mr. Washington apologizes for injustice . . . does not rightly value the privilege and duty of voting . . . and opposes the higher training and ambition of our brighter minds—so far as he, the South, or the Nation, does this—we must unceasingly and firmly oppose them.

Du Bois argued that the African American community should try to develop what he called "the talented tenth." That is, it should find ways to transform the most able ten percent of the black population into intellectual leaders. They could then help the rest of the African American population.

Rise of the NAACP

In the early 1890s, the country was suffering financially. The lives of African Americans took a turn for the worse. Jim Crow laws had resulted in separate facilities for white people and black people. The Supreme Court actually supported these laws in a court case. The court's decision in *Plessy v. Ferguson* declared that segregation was legal, so long as equal facilities were available to both African Americans and white people. In reality, the "equal facilities" were rarely equal. But many Americans were willing to look the other way. Even some reformers who were "progressive" on other issues raised no objection to Jim Crow laws. As if this were not enough, lynchings and race-related riots were increasing, and not only in the South.

In response to this violence and loss of civil rights, a group called the Niagara Movement formed. It first met in 1905. The group, led by Du Bois, met in Niagara Falls, Canada, because its African American members were not welcome in the hotels of nearby Buffalo, New York. The group called for an end to racial discrimination and full civil rights for African Americans.

Many white reformers also opposed the way African Americans were being treated. Over time, these white reformers joined with many of those in the Niagara Movement. They formed the National Association for the Advancement of Colored People (NAACP). This group became a leader in the national civil rights movement.

For many years, Du Bois was the leader of the NAACP. Eventually, however, Du Bois grew discouraged by the continuing racial inequality in the United States. He moved to the African nation of Ghana and became a member of the Communist Party. Du Bois died in Ghana in August 1963.

In 1905 a group of African Americans founded the Niagara Movement to call for an end to racial discrimination and fight for full civil rights for African Americans. In this photograph of the founding group, W.E. B. Du Bois is seated in the center of the middle row.

March on Washington

Although Du Bois himself grew disenchanted with the United States, his work in this country did eventually bear fruit. The civil rights movement of the 1950s and 1960s won an end to segregation, including a 1954 Supreme Court decision that declared separate was, by definition, unequal. As result, schools throughout the South were forced to **integrate**.

Then, on the day after Du Bois died, August 28, 1963, more than two hundred thousand people gathered in Washington, D.C. They came to hear leaders of the NAACP and other organizations

Vocabulary

integrate, v. to end a policy that keeps apart people of different races; to make a place open to everyone

speak out for equal civil rights for all Americans. They also came to demonstrate support for civil rights legislation that was pending in Congress.

During this "March on Washington," thousands of people marched to the Lincoln Memorial. From the steps of the memorial, Dr. Martin Luther King Jr. gave his famous "I Have a Dream" speech. "I have a dream," King said, "that one day this nation will rise up and live out the true meaning of its creed: 'We hold these truths to be self-evident, that all men are created equal.'"

The civil rights movement of the 1960s had many successes. It pushed state and federal governments to pass laws against racial discrimination and to guarantee African Americans equal rights. But the successes of the 1960s would have been impossible without the pioneering work of the people you have just read about, as well as hundreds of others like them who were willing to speak out—and even die—for equal rights.

During the March on Washington for Jobs and Freedom, which took place on August 28, 1963, civil rights leader Dr. Martin Luther King Jr. delivered his famous "I Have a Dream" speech.

Chapter 6
Women's Voting Rights

The Story Behind the Vote Imagine that your teacher has said that you will have class elections, but only half of the class—the girls—will be allowed to participate. The other half will not be allowed to vote. How would that make you feel? If you were a boy, you would probably howl in protest!

The Big Question

What causes did American women fight for in the 1800s, and what actions did they take to gain the right to vote?

Until the first quarter of the 1900s, women in the United States faced a situation like the one just described. Most of them were not allowed to vote, and most were discouraged from even discussing political issues in public. Although the Declaration of Independence proclaimed that "all men are created equal" and endowed with certain "**unalienable rights**," voting rights and other political rights were not generally extended to women. In 1900, only a handful of western states allowed women to vote.

Vocabulary

"unalienable right," (phrase) a legal promise that cannot be taken away or denied

It may surprise you to learn that in a couple of the original colonies, Massachusetts and New Jersey, women were allowed to vote in town meetings, or if they were the head of a household. But these rights were later taken away.

By and large, in the early 1900s, women in America did not have the right to vote.

During the early years of American history, a number of women raised their voices to complain about these inequalities, including Abigail Adams, the wife of the second president, John Adams. You may also be familiar with some other early advocates of women's rights. Susan B. Anthony, Elizabeth Cady Stanton, Lucretia Mott, and the African American activist Sojourner Truth all fought for women's rights in the 1800s.

Several of these women attended the Seneca Falls Convention in 1848. There they passed resolutions seeking equality with men. Throughout the second half of the 1800s, they continued to work on behalf of women. Yet they failed to achieve their main goal—the right to vote.

Susan B. Anthony (left) and Elizabeth Cady Stanton (right) were close partners in the women's voting rights movement.

The movement that sought to secure women's right to vote was known as the woman **suffrage** movement. Those who fought for the cause were known as *suffragists,* or (when they were women) *suffragettes*. One of the most famous of the suffragettes was Susan B. Anthony.

Susan B. Anthony

Susan Brownell Anthony was born in 1820 and raised in a **Quaker** household. Her father supported her interest in education. In the Quaker tradition, women were expected to play an active role in the church. They were invited to speak their minds about church issues. Many Quakers were also involved in political causes of the day, especially the abolitionist movement—a movement against slavery—and the temperance movement—a movement against the excessive drinking of alcohol. Susan B. Anthony was exposed to both of these movements as a young woman.

As a young woman, Anthony also paid attention to the conditions of many married women around her. Although she had many suitors, she decided that she would not marry. Many years later she said, "I never felt I could give up my life of freedom to become a man's housekeeper. When I was young if a girl married poverty, she became a drudge; if she married wealth, she became a doll. Had I married at twenty-one, I would have been either a drudge or a doll for fifty-five years. Think of it!"

After teaching school for several years, Anthony was looking for a different challenge. Her father encouraged her to take up a social cause and not to concern herself with earning a living. At the time, some women of her social class were volunteering to work as religious missionaries. Missionaries traveled to promote their particular religion. Others were becoming involved in the temperance and abolitionist movements.

Susan B. Anthony was born in Adams, Massachusetts, in 1820. This is the house where she was born.

Susan B. Anthony's family knew many famous abolitionists of the day. Her brother was a friend of John Brown, whose antislavery actions had caused months of upheaval and several deaths in Kansas. Anthony admired the abolitionists. But she found another cause even more appealing. She wanted to help women gain rights.

For a time, Susan B. Anthony worked in the temperance movement. Many women took up the cause of temperance because they saw how alcohol abuse led to the breakdown of family life, immoral behavior, and unemployment. In 1852, Anthony went as a delegate to a meeting of temperance workers. When she attempted to speak, the chairman told her, "The sisters were not invited to speak, but to listen and learn."

Frustrated by the fact that women were not permitted to speak publicly, Anthony walked out of the convention. She was followed by a handful of other women. They formed their own organization, the Women's State Temperance Society. In this group, they could speak and be heard by other women.

Women in particular spoke out against alcohol abuse and the many problems this caused.

"Outrageous Behavior"

Later that year, the new organization sent Susan B. Anthony and Amelia Bloomer to a convention of the Men's State Temperance Society. Proper gentlemen were outraged when the two female delegates walked in. Both were wearing pants under their skirts, and Susan B. Anthony had cut her hair. This behavior seemed outrageous to many of the delegates. In the uproar that followed, the women were ruled out of order when they tried to speak. The pants the women wore to the convention later became very fashionable and were called "bloomers" after Amelia Bloomer.

"Bloomers" were named after Amelia Bloomer, who caused an outrage when she wore full pants under her skirts.

Finally, Susan B. Anthony understood what many women reformers had recognized a decade earlier. Before women could be effective in bringing about change in society, they must first obtain equal political rights for themselves. From this point forward, Anthony dedicated her life to securing women's political rights—especially the right to vote.

Anthony was such a good organizer and leader that she came to be known as the Napoleon of the women's rights movement. While Anthony was well organized and had no trouble attending to details like publicity and planning meetings, she herself detested public speaking. Despite this, she spoke publicly when she had to.

The Fourteenth Amendment

After the Civil War, many men and women in the women's rights movement turned their energies to the support of African Americans who had been freed under the Thirteenth Amendment. The reformers, however, disagreed about how to proceed. Many men felt that freed men should be given the right to vote as soon as possible. The Fourteenth Amendment had been proposed, and when passed by Congress and **ratified** by the states, would make African American men citizens and grant them the right to vote.

> **Vocabulary**
> **ratify,** v. to approve

Elizabeth Cady Stanton discovered that the wording in the Fourteenth Amendment would extend voting rights only to "male inhabitants." She wanted the amendment to be rewritten so that women, too, would be included.

As Stanton, Anthony, and other women fought to include their rights in the amendment, along with those of the newly freed people, many men urged them to wait. They felt that the issues of African American and woman suffrage were both unpopular. Trying to push both changes through at once would reduce the likelihood of either one passing. Stanton and Anthony were unsuccessful in their efforts to change the wording of the Fourteenth Amendment.

Against their better judgment, the women waited and watched as the Fourteenth Amendment was ratified—without including their interests.

Some people, however, including members of government, thought the new amendment could be interpreted as also including women in the right to vote. In 1872, Anthony decided to challenge the amendment. The first section of the amendment reads:

> All persons born or **naturalized** in the United States . . . are citizens. . . . No State shall make or enforce any law which shall abridge [limit] the privileges . . . of citizens.

Only a small section later on mentioned that this was limited to men. In the next election, Susan B. Anthony and her sisters placed their ballots in the ballot box. (A ballot was a slip of paper on which a person selected, or voted for, their chosen candidate.) A few weeks later, Anthony and a handful of other women were arrested for voting illegally. Anthony refused to post **bail**, money that would have allowed her to stay out of jail, but her lawyer paid her bail. Anthony hoped to push the matter into the courts.

The judge who heard the case was not sympathetic. It was his first case, and he did not even allow Anthony to be called as a witness on her own behalf. As soon as the opposing attorney finished speaking, the judge pulled a piece of paper from his pocket announcing his decision. He had written it even before hearing the facts of the case! He ruled against Susan B. Anthony.

In her defense, Anthony wrote:

> Friends and fellow citizens: I stand before you tonight under **indictment** for the alleged crime of having voted at the last presidential election, without having a lawful right to vote. It shall be my work this evening

to prove to you that in thus voting, I not only committed no crime, but, instead, simply exercised my citizen's rights, guaranteed to me and all United States citizens by the National Constitution, beyond the power of any state to deny.

The preamble of the Federal Constitution says: "We, the people of the United States, in order to form a more perfect union, establish justice, insure domestic tranquillity, provide for the common defense, promote the general welfare, and secure the blessings of liberty to ourselves and our posterity, do ordain and establish this Constitution for the United States of America."

It was we, the people; not we, the white male citizens . . . . but we, the whole people, who formed the Union. And we formed it, not to give the blessings of liberty, but to secure them; not to the half of ourselves

Women campaigned across the country for the right to vote.

and the half of our posterity, but to the whole people—women as well as men. . . .

Webster, Worcester, and Bouvier [famous dictionary makers] all define a citizen to be a person in the United States, entitled to vote and hold office.

The only question left to be seeded now is: Are women persons? And I hardly believe any of our opponents will have the hardihood [nerve; guts] to say they are not.

More Battles

After Anthony's failure in court, many women turned their efforts back toward the temperance movement. This angered the makers of beer and whiskey. These businesses began to buy votes to fight against woman suffrage. Immigrants also were urged to keep women from voting. Political bosses feared that if women got the right to vote, changes would take place in the practices that made these bosses rich and powerful.

The bosses used bribery and illegal voting by immigrant men to work against woman suffrage. Many of these immigrants came from countries where women's rights were taken even less seriously than they were in the United States, so they were not hard to persuade.

Susan B. Anthony persevered in spite of this resistance. She continued to write articles and lecture around the country. Anthony served as president of the National American Woman Suffrage Association from 1892 to 1900. Each year, suffragists tried to send a new bill to Congress. Each year it failed to pass.

Susan B. Anthony never gave up hope that American women would soon secure their right to vote. A few weeks before her death in 1906, she noted, "Failure is impossible."

Despite her many decades of work, she did not live to see passage of the amendment that allows women to vote.

The suffrage movement grew and strengthened across America and other parts of the world. In this photograph, taken in 1917, women are protesting for the right to vote on the steps of the U.S. Capitol Building.

The Nineteenth Amendment

The hopes for women's right to vote did not die with Susan B. Anthony. A battle took place to add an amendment to the Constitution that would guarantee the right of women to vote. Eventually, this effort would result in the passage and ratification of the Nineteenth Amendment.

Leaders in other areas of civil rights fights also supported the Nineteenth Amendment. W E. B. Du Bois wrote that every African American man should vote in favor of woman suffrage.

Around the country, other supporters of woman suffrage held silent protests, went on hunger strikes, and organized parades.

A few more states approved women's right to vote. When New York State passed a law allowing women to vote in 1917, President Woodrow Wilson decided he would no longer oppose the movement. Times were changing.

It was an era of reform. More people began to believe that women would help clean up policies. Their votes would help protect families. Congress was less likely to fight an amendment for women's right to vote.

In 1918, Jeannette Rankin of Montana, the first woman elected to Congress, introduced the Nineteenth Amendment. It got the necessary two-thirds vote in Congress during June 1919, passing by one vote. Some members of Congress who were ill left the hospital to be counted. One congressman left his wife's deathbed to vote on the issue. The amendment was then submitted to the states for ratification before becoming law.

The Nineteenth Amendment to the Constitution was ratified by three-fourths of the states on August 18, 1920, and became law. The wording was exactly as Anthony had proposed years before:

> The right of citizens of the United States to vote shall not be denied or abridged by the United States or by any State on account of sex.
>
> Congress shall have power to enforce this article by appropriate legislation.

In this photograph, the governor of Nevada is seen ratifying the Nineteenth Amendment to the Constitution in 1920.

Chapter 7
Eugene Debs and Socialism

Ripe for Reform Throughout the later 1800s and early 1900s, reformers continued to work to improve the lives of people all across the United States—from farmers to immigrants.

The Big Question

What were Eugene Debs's political beliefs?

These groups and many others had fewer privileges and less power than the middle class and the wealthy people who ran industry and government at the time. In trying to improve lives, many reformers followed the principles of socialism. Socialism, you may recall, was an economic system in which the government controlled or regulated major, or important, industries.

Eugene Debs

Eugene Debs, son of a Midwestern grocer, rose to lead the Socialist Party in the United States. He ran for president as the Social Democratic candidate in five elections. He received nearly a million votes on his third try, in 1912.

Debs identified with all poor and downtrodden people. He summed up his philosophy in these words: "While there is a lower class, I am in it. While there is a criminal element, I am of it. While there is a soul in prison, I am not free."

Eugene Debs was the presidential candidate of the Socialist Party five times.

Debs was born in 1855 to immigrant parents from France. He finished his schooling at the age of fourteen or fifteen and went to work for a railroad company. Despite his lack of a formal education, Debs was widely read. His family exposed him to many classics of French and German literature. His first job at the railroad was scraping grease and paint off locomotives. He earned fifty cents a day. After working in the railroad shops, Debs became a railroad fireman—the person who shoveled coal into the furnace of a steam locomotive.

Debs quickly proved himself a leader. He started a local branch of the Brotherhood of Locomotive Firemen, a railroad union. He edited the union magazine. He also served in local government. Soon Debs worked for the union on a national level. He also served in the Indiana legislature.

Debs and other union leaders did not always see eye to eye on all issues. Samuel Gompers was an important labor leader in the late 1800s and early 1900s. Gompers worked to organize workers of different trade unions into one large labor organization called the American Federation of Labor (AFL).

Debs opposed Gompers's plan. He preferred to organize the workers within an industry into a single union, despite the different jobs they might have in the industry. His belief was that this would keep unions of different crafts in the same overall industry from competing with each other on labor issues. Debs formed one such union himself, called the American Railway Union.

The Pullman Strike

In the late 1800s, there were many workers' strikes. One of the worst of these was a strike against the Pullman Car Company.

George Pullman's company made railroad cars. Pullman cars were designed to make travel more comfortable. They had special features for sleeping and dining. In 1894, workers at the Pullman Company went on strike.

This photograph shows a lounge car inside a Pullman train.

The striking workers were protesting layoffs and pay cuts. Pullman took these actions because his business was suffering as a result of a depression. This was the same depression that caused the unrest among farmers. It hit the nation hard.

The Pullman Strike led to violent riots in Chicago. Trains were vandalized. Some people were shot. Debs was a leader in one of the unions on strike. He was arrested and imprisoned.

Turn to Socialism

Debs came to believe that unions would never be strong enough to protect the rights of workers. He thought that only a different economic system from the one the United States had would achieve this goal. Later, Debs described how the Pullman riots in 1894 and his prison experience shaped his political views:

> [During the strike] an army of detectives, thugs, and murderers were equipped [by the railroad owners and local authorities] with badge[s] and bludgeon[s] [clubs] and turned loose [on the strikers]; old hulks of [railroad] cars were [set on fire]; the alarm bells tolled [rang]; the people were terrified; . . . the [telegraph] wires sped the news that Chicago's white throat was in the clutch of a red [socialist or communist] mob; injunctions [court orders to stop doing something] flew thick and fast, arrests followed, and our office and headquarters, the heart of the strike, was sacked [looted], torn out and nailed up by the "lawful" authorities of the federal government; and when in company with my loyal comrades I found myself in Cook County jail at Chicago with the whole press screaming conspiracy, treason and murder.

The Pullman Strike helped convince Debs that the U.S. government needed to be changed—in the direction of socialism.

At the time, public opinion about Debs, strikes, and unions was sharply divided. Theodore Roosevelt called Debs an "undesirable citizen." Samuel Gompers, while supporting the railroad strikers, refused to have the AFL take part in the strike. Others called Debs the nation's best speaker and writer on labor issues. For several years, Debs would be a leader not just in the labor efforts but also in the socialist movement in the United States.

Striking workers disrupted the railroads for several months during the Pullman Strike.

The Wobblies

In 1905, Eugene Debs helped form the Industrial Workers of the World (IWW). This group of skilled and unskilled workers was dedicated to the overthrow of capitalism. Members of the IWW were called "Wobblies." (No one is sure why they got this name.) Some Wobblies were in favor of violent acts to achieve their goals. Debs soon left the organization because he disapproved of its acceptance of violent tactics.

Socialism Peaks

Socialism in the United States has probably never been stronger than it was in the early 1900s. Such socialist ideas had grown out of the American labor movement of the 1830s and 1840s. Further ideas arrived in America along with the millions of immigrants. But some immigrants were disappointed by what they found in America. Many lived in the sort of poverty that Jacob Riis and Jane Addams worked to end, and many were attracted by the principles of socialism advocated by Eugene Debs. These immigrants and other poor people felt that Debs was a political candidate they could trust.

Debs ran for president several times as a Socialist Party candidate. His first campaign was in 1900. He toured the country, making speeches against capitalism. His words convinced many people to vote for him. In the election of 1912, Eugene Debs got 6 percent of the vote for president. Although this was not a high percentage of the total vote, Debs's success convinced other politicians to begin addressing the issues raised by socialism. Reform-minded candidates, including Debs, had shared about 75 percent of the vote. This figure proved that the reform movements of the Progressive Era had gained widespread acceptance and begun to have an impact on the lives of Americans.

While imprisoned for illegally encouraging a rail strike, Eugene Debs was nominated to be a presidential candidate on the Socialist ticket. He ran several times. This is a poster from the 1904 campaign.

The Canton Speech

At the beginning of World War I, it seemed that
the United States would be able to stay out of the
conflict, but in 1917, the United States entered
the war. To silence opposition to participating
in the war, Congress passed the **Espionage** Act,
forbidding people to speak out against the war.
But the act did not silence Eugene Debs.

As the war raged, Debs insisted on speaking out against it. In 1918, he
delivered an address called the "Canton Speech." In the speech, Debs
reviewed many of the issues that he had spoken about earlier in his career.
He talked about capitalism as one of the causes of the war and complained
about the burden of the war on workers. He also spoke in praise of socialism:

> Socialism is a growing idea; an expanding philosophy. It is spreading
> over the entire face of the earth: It is as vain to resist it as it would be to
> arrest the sunrise on the morrow. It is coming, coming, coming all along
> the line.

Debs's speech was powerful, but under the Espionage Act, it was considered
treason. Debs was arrested and later sentenced to ten years in prison for
speaking his mind. But being in jail didn't stop the activist from running for
the presidency again in 1920. One of Debs's campaign slogans was, "From the
jailhouse to the White House."

In 1921, two years after Debs was imprisoned, President Warren G. Harding
ordered his release. Debs continued to speak out—this time against the
unequal treatment in jails of African Americans and poor prisoners compared
to other prisoners.

Debs ran for president of the United States five times in all. His last campaign
failed in 1920. Although he was never elected, his influence was substantial.

Even though he was behind bars, Eugene ran for the office of president.

He wrote widely on issues such as racial injustice, and he supported woman suffrage and the concept of equal wages for equal work.

Debs also supported the National Association for the Advancement of Colored People in its crusade against Jim Crow laws. He defended free speech and helped start the American Civil Liberties Union (ACLU), a group that aimed (and still aims) to defend the constitutional rights of American citizens. Finally a life of struggle took its toll on Debs's health, and he died in 1926.

Intertwined Lives

The lives of the social reformers you have read about were all intertwined. William Jennings Bryan and Jane Addams had faced each other as members of college debating teams. Theodore Roosevelt worked with Jacob Riis to correct the abuses that were common in New York City's homeless shelters. Booker T. Washington, Ida B. Wells, and W E. B. Du Bois held long debates about the best ways to secure a better life for African Americans. Jane Addams worked with Du Bois and others in forming the NAACP.

The reformers were able to accomplish so much in improving the lives of everyday people in part because they pulled together on so many issues. They proved that a group of individuals working together can do more than any one person can do alone.

Glossary

A

antiquities, n. objects from ancient times (200)

B

bail, n. money posted to free a prisoner until his or her trial begins (229)

brewery, n. a factory that produces beer (178)

boycott, n. a form of organized protest in which people refuse to buy goods or have anything to do with a particular group or country (208)

C

capitalism, n. an economic system in which resources and businesses are privately owned and prices are not controlled by the government (166)

"cholera epidemic," (phrase) a situation in which cholera, a serious bacterial infection of the intestine, spreads to many people in an area or region (184)

civil rights, n. certain rights, such as the right to vote, or the right to a fair trial, that are guaranteed by the Constitution and its amendments to all American citizens (206)

compromise, n. when each side in a dispute gives up some of their demands to reach an agreement (215)

conservationist, n. a person who wants to stop human actions that are harmful to wild or natural spaces (200)

D

depression, n. an extended period of reduced economic activity, when large numbers of people cannot find jobs and most people have less money to spend (183)

E

espionage, n. spying (241)

F

free trade, n. a policy of unrestricted trade, in which the government does not use quotas, tariffs, or other measures to regulate imports and exports (170)

G

gold standard, n. the use of the country's supply of gold to back up the value of paper money (158)

H

humanitarian, adj. caring about the well-being of all people (209)

I

indictment, n. a formal written accusation of a crime (229)

inflation, n. a rise in prices and a fall in the purchasing value of money (156)

integrate, v. to end a policy that keeps apart people of different races; to make a place open to everyone (220)

L

landmark, n. an area or a structure that has special significance (200)

legislation, n. laws made by a government (180)

legislature, n. the government body responsible for making laws (175)

lynching, n. the killing of a person by a mob, often by hanging (208)

M

meatpacking, adj. related to the business of processing, packing, and distributing meat (167)

N

natural resource, n. something from nature that is useful to humans (198)

naturalist, n. an expert in natural history; a person who studies nature (200)

naturalized, adj. having gained citizenship in a new country (229)

O

oil-refining, adj. related to purifying petroleum (oil) to produce a product for sale (167)

P

political party, n. a group of people who work together to elect government officials and direct government policies (154)

populist, adj. reflecting the beliefs of people who fight for the rights and interests of the common people (154)

"Progressive Era," (phrase) a time of social and political activism in the United States during the early 1900s, characterized by changes and reforms aimed at improving people's lives (166)

Q

Quaker, n. a member of a Christian religious group called the Society of Friends, which encourages people to work for justice (225)

R

ratify, v. to approve (228)

"regulatory body," (phrase) a governmental group that has authority or control over an area of activity, usually for the purpose of protecting the public (197)

running mate, n. a political partner also running for office (194)

S

sanitation, n. the system of keeping a place clean and free of disease (186)

"second the nomination," (phrase) agree with the proposal to appoint or elect a person for something (182)

secretary of state, n. the U.S. government official in charge of helping the president in his dealings with foreign countries (162)

segregate, v. to keep people separate, usually on the basis of race (206)

segregation, n. the act of keeping people separate, usually on the basis of race (152)

social class, n. a group of people who share a similar way of life and level of importance or influence in society (178)

suffrage, n. the right to vote (225)

T

trade union, n. an organization formed by workers with a specific skill, such as electricians, to win and protect their rights; today the term is used interchangeably with *labor union* (157)

treason, n. disloyalty to a country by helping an enemy (241)

trust, n. a combination of corporations created to reduce competition and control prices (170)

U

"unalienable right," (phrase) a legal promise that cannot be taken away or denied (222)

Core Knowledge®

CKHG™
Core Knowledge HISTORY AND GEOGRAPHY™

Series Editor-In-Chief
E.D. Hirsch, Jr.

Editorial Directors
Linda Bevilacqua and Rosie McCormick

Immigration

Subject Matter Expert

J. Chris Arndt, PhD, Department of History, James Madison University

Tony Williams, Senior Teaching Fellow, Bill of Rights Institute

Illustration and Photo Credits

Industrialization and Urbanization in America

Subject Matter Expert

J. Chris Arndt, PhD, Department of History, James Madison University

Tony Williams, Senior Teaching Fellow, Bill of Rights Institute

Illustration and Photo Credits

4X5 Collection/SuperStock: 95

A lady typist at work (b/w photo), English photographer, (20th century) (after)/Private Collection/© Look and Learn/Bridgeman Images: 117

Arriving of immigrants in Ellis Island, New York, c. 1905/Photo © PVDE/Bridgeman Images: 147

Art Archive, The/SuperStock: 113

Breaker boys (who sort coal by hand) at Hughestown Borough Coal Co. Pittston, Pennsylvania, 1911 (b/w photo), Hine, Lewis Wickes (1874–1940)/Private Collection/Bridgeman Images: 114

Breaker boys in a coal mine, Pittston, Pennsylvania, USA, 1911 (b/w photo) , Hine, Lewis Wickes (1874–1940)/Private Collection/J. T. Vintage/Bridgeman Images: 114

Broad Street and Curb Brokers, New York City, USA, c.1910 (b/w photo)/Circa Images/Bridgeman Images: 133

Campus, University of Chicago (coloured photo), American Photographer (19th century) (after)/Private Collection/© Look and Learn/Bridgeman Images: 105

Cartoon featuring William Marcy 'Boss' Tweed (1823–78) from 'Harper's Weekly', 6th January 1872 (coloured engraving), Nast, Thomas (1840–1902)/Private Collection/Peter Newark American Pictures/Bridgeman Images: 144

Child Arriving At Ellis Island (b/w photo)/Underwood Archives/UIG/Bridgeman Images: 147

Circa Images/Glasshouse Images/SuperStock: 138–139

Coal mine, 1906 : miner with a lamp and child/Bridgeman Images: 74

Doffers replacing full bobbins at Indian Orchard Cotton Mill, Massachusetts, 1916 (b/w photo), Hine, Lewis Wickes (1874–1940)/Private Collection/Bridgeman Images: 52–53

Everett Collection/SuperStock: 62–63, 82, 91, 122

Glasshouse Images/SuperStock: 94

Going Through the Form of Universal Suffrage, 1871 (wood engraving), Nast, Thomas (1840–1902)/Collection of the New-York Historical Society, USA/Bridgeman Images: 146

Hand spinning, carding and roving, 1848/Universal History Archive/UIG/Bridgeman Images: 57

Heinz Tschanz-Hofmann/SuperStock: 91

High angle view of a freight train moving on railroad track/Bridgeman Images: 106

Illustrated London News Ltd/Pantheon/SuperStock: 142

Immigrant children arriving in New York/Universal History Archive/UIG/Bridgeman Images: 147

Immigrants on Ellis Island reception centre, 1902/Universal History Archive/UIG/Bridgeman Images: 147

Immigrants served a free meal at Ellis Island, c.1906 (b/w photo), Levick, Edwin (1868–1929)/New York Public Library, USA/Bridgeman Images: 147

Men working in the W. 129th Street sewer, New York, c.1911 (b/w photo), Hassler, William Davis (1877–1921)/Collection of the New-York Historical Society, USA/Bridgeman Images: 141

New York Stock Exchange (photo)/Buyenlarge Archive/UIG/Bridgeman Images: 77

Oil City, 1872/© SZ Photo/Bridgeman Images: 69

Oil refinery in Richmond, 1912 (b/w photo)/© SZ Photo/Bridgeman Images: 100–101

One of the smallest apprentices I found. (Work being slack.) De Pedro Casellas Cigar Factory, Tampa, FL 1909 (photo)/Universal History Archive/UIG/Bridgeman Images: 123

Paraffin lamp/Dorling Kindersley/UIG/Bridgeman Images: 96

Past Pix/Science and Society/SuperStock: 111

Peter Sickles/SuperStock: 51, 88–89

Portrait of Alexander Graham Bell speaking into a telephone receiver, c.1876 (photo)/Private Collection/Prismatic Pictures/Bridgeman Images: 80

Portrait of Cornelius Vanderbilt/Underwood Archives/UIG/Bridgeman Images: 65

Portrait of John D. Rockefeller aged 18, 1857 (b/w photo), American Photographer, (19th century)/Private Collection/Prismatic Pictures/Bridgeman Images: 97

Registration of immigrants, 1928 (b/w photo)/© SZ Photo/Scherl/Bridgeman Images: 147

Rush Hour Traffic in Washington, DC packs trolley cars 1919 (photo)/Universal History Archive/UIG/Bridgeman Images: 137

Russian immigrant family in Ellis Island, 1929 (b/w photo)/© SZ Photo/Scherl/Bridgeman Images: 147

Science and Society/SuperStock: 79

Seeing Chicago, auto at Monroe near State, Chicago, Illinois, 1900 (b/w photo), Behm, Hans (fl.1900–10)/Private Collection/Bridgeman : 128–129

Shoppers and Elevated Train Along Sixth Avenue, New York City, USA, c.1903 (b/w photo)/Circa Images/Bridgeman Images: 137

Soap Trust. No! Blowed if I'll use it, I'll go dirty first (colour litho), English School, (20th century)/Private Collection/© Look and Learn/Elgar Collection/Bridgeman Images: 104

Steel industry in the USA, 1938 (b/w photo)/© SZ Photo/Scherl/Bridgeman Images: 67

Stockyards, Kansas City, Missouri, USA, c.1906 (b/w photo)/Circa Images/Bridgeman Images: 131

The cobbler (b/w photo), English photographer, (20th century) (after)/Private Collection/© Look and Learn/Valerie Jackson Harris Collection/Bridgeman Images: 108–109

The Doubling Room, Dean Mills, 1851 (colour litho), English School, (19th century)/Private Collection/Bridgeman Images: 60

The first cotton mill in America, established by Samuel Slater on the Blackstone River at Pawtucket, Rhode Island, c.1790 (oil on canvas), American School, (18th century)/Smithsonian Institution, Washington DC, USA/Bridgeman Images: 58

The horse-car, early 1900s (b/w photo), American Photographer, (20th century)/Private Collection/The Stapleton Collection/Bridgeman Images: 135

The Labour-Fight at the Carnegie Steelworks, Homestead, Pennsylvania, from 'The Graphic', 30th July 1892 (litho), English School, (19th century)/Private Collection/Peter Newark American Pictures/Bridgeman Images: 127

The Wealth of England: the Bessemer Process of Making Steel', 1895 (oil on canvas), Titcomb, William Holt Yates (1858–1930)/Kelham Island Industrial Museum, Sheffield, UK/Bridgeman Images: 92

Thomas Edison in his laboratory./Universal History Archive/UIG/Bridgeman Images: 87

Thomas Edison in his workshop (colour litho), Cameron, John (1830–76) (after)/Private Collection/The Stapleton Collection/Bridgeman Images: 85

Thomas Edison/Bridgeman Images: 83

Transcontinental Railroad (b/w photo)/Underwood Archives/UIG/Bridgeman Images: 65

Underwood Photo Archives/SuperStock: 125

View Pictures Ltd/SuperStock: 99

Westend61/SuperStock: 92

When They Were Young: Thomas Edison - the American inventor, Jackson, Peter (1922–2003)/Private Collection/© Look and Learn/Bridgeman Images: 81

Women strikers, ready to confront the men in the mines, 1891 (colour litho), American School, (19th century)/Schlesinger Library, Radcliffe Institute, Harvard University/Bridgeman Images: 119

Work at a Coal Mine, II (engraving), Nash, Joseph (d.1922)/Private Collection/© Look and Learn/Illustrated Papers Collection/Bridgeman Images: 73

World History Archive/SuperStock: 54, 112

Reform in Industrial America

Subject Matter Expert

J. Chris Arndt, PhD, Department of History, James Madison University

Tony Williams, Senior Teaching Fellow, Bill of Rights Institute

Illustration and Photo Credits

Bandits' Roost / Universal History Archive/UIG / Bridgeman Images: 187

Birthplace of Susan B. Anthony, 1899 / Universal History Archive/UIG / Bridgeman Images: 226

Booker T. Washington, Seated Portrait, Washington DC, USA, Harris & Ewing, January 1909 (b/w photo) / Circa Images / Bridgeman Images: 210

Campaign poster for William Mckinley (1843–1901) as President and Theodore Roosevelt (1858–1919) as Vice-President, 1900 (colour litho), American School, (20th century) / Private Collection / Peter Newark American Pictures / Bridgeman Images: 194

Cartoon of Theodore 'Teddy' Roosevelt refusing to shoot a bear cub, 1902 (litho), Berryman, Clifford K. (1869–1949) (after) / Private Collection / Peter Newark American Pictures / Bridgeman Images: 197

Circa Images/Glasshouse Images/SuperStock: 164–165, 222–223

Colonel Roosevelt and his Rough Riders at the top of the hill which they captured, Battle of San Juan 1898 (photo) / Universal History Archive/ UIG / Bridgeman Images: 193

Eugene Victor "Gene" Debs / Universal History Archive/UIG / Bridgeman Images: 235

Eugene Victor Debs (1855–1926) Campaign Poster of 1920 (b/w photo), American Photographer, (20th century) / Private Collection / Peter Newark American Pictures / Bridgeman Images: 242

Everett Collection/SuperStock: 151, 221, 230, 232, 233, 239

Front Cover of 'Twenty Years at Hull House' by Jane Addams, 1910 (colour litho), American School, (20th century) / Newberry Library, Chicago, Illinois, USA / Bridgeman Images: 181

I Feed You All, 1875 / Universal History Archive/UIG / Bridgeman Images: 154

Iberfoto/SuperStock: 179

Illustrated London News Ltd/ Pantheon/SuperStock: 174

Jacob Riis (photo) / Universal History Archive/UIG / Bridgeman Images: 185

Jeff Greenberg/age fotostock/SuperStock: 201

John Coletti/Jon Arnold Images/SuperStock: 218

Library of Congress, Prints and Photographs Division, LC-DIG-ppmsca-37818: 220

Lounge car, Midwest MS Pullman, 4025 Fontain Club, 1932 (b/w photo), American Photographer, (20th century) / Newberry Library, Chicago, Illinois, USA / Bridgeman Images: 237

Male and Female Students Reading at Tables in Library, Tuskegee Institute, Tuskegee, Alabama, USA, 1902 (b/w photo), Johnson, Frances Benjamin (fl.c.1900–1925) / Circa Images / Bridgeman Images: 214

McClure's Magazine Cover, USA, 1910s / © The Advertising Archives / Bridgeman Images: 168

Members of the National Christian Temperance Union singing hymns and praying for lost souls in a saloon, 1874 (engraving), American School, (19th century) / Private Collection / Peter Newark Historical Pictures / Bridgeman Images: 227

National Geographic/SuperStock: 199, 201

Pantheon/SuperStock: 227

Portrait of Ida B. Wells Barnett, c.1893 (sepia photo), American School, (19th century) / Private Collection / Prismatic Pictures / Bridgeman Images: 207

Portrait of Jane Addams, c.1901 (photo) / Private Collection / Prismatic Pictures / Bridgeman Images: 177

Portrait of John D. Rockefeller in his older years (b/w photo), American Photographer, (20th century) / Private Collection / The Stapleton Collection / Bridgeman Images: 169

President Theodore Roosevelt standing on a reviewing stand, 1904 / Universal History Archive/UIG / Bridgeman Images: 196

Robert C. Ogden, Senator William Howard Taft, Booker T. Washington and Andrew Carnegie. / Universal History Archive/UIG / Bridgeman Images: 216

Roof Construction by Students at Tuskegee Institute, Tuskegee, Alabama, USA, 1902 (b/w photo), Johnson, Frances Benjamin (fl.c.1900–1925) / Circa Images / Bridgeman Images: 214

Segregation Sign at Greyhound Bus Terminal on Trip from Louisville, Kentucky, to Memphis, Tennessee, USA, Esther Bubley for Office of War Information, September 1943 / Circa Images / Bridgeman Images: 205

Silver certificate banknote / Universal History Archive/UIG / Bridgeman Images: 156

Spinner (Addie Laird), 1910 (gelatin silver print), Hine, Lewis Wickes (1874–1940) / Private Collection / Photo © Christie's Images / Bridgeman Images: 153

Susan B. Anthony, Elizabeth Cady Stanton, 1899 / Universal History Archive/UIG / Bridgeman Images: 224

Teddy Roosevelt and John Muir (b/w photo) / Underwood Archives/UIG / Bridgeman Images: 200

The Lincoln gates, Tuskegee Institute, Ala. 1906 (photo) / Universal History Archive/UIG / Bridgeman Images: 213

The Octopus Who Strangles the World, cartoon from 'The Minneapolis Times', reproduced in 'Lectures Pour Tous', 1902–03 (engraving) (b/w photo), American School, (20th century) / Private Collection / Archives Charmet / Bridgeman Images: 171

The Socialist Party Presidential Ticket of 1904, 1904 (lithograph), American School, (20th century) / Private Collection / Photo © GraphicaArtis / Bridgeman Images: 240

Theodore Roosevelt (1858–1919) here as a child on horse c. 1870 / Bridgeman Images: 190–191

Theodore Roosevelt campaigning as the Progressive Bull moose party candidate for President in the summer of 1912 oil over a photo / Bridgeman Images: 183

Theodore Roosevelt smiling from an automobile (b/w photo) / Private Collection / Bridgeman Images: 203

Two Young Girls Working in Hosiery Mill, Loudon, Tennessee, USA, circa 1910 / Circa Images / Bridgeman Images: 188

Universal Images Group/SuperStock: 211

USA: William Howard Taft (1857–1930) was the 27th President of the United States, serving from 1909 to 1913. Photographic portrait, March 1909 / Pictures from History / Bridgeman Images: 202

William Edward Burghardt Du Bois (1868–1963) 1904 (b&w photo) / Private Collection / Bridgeman Images: 210

William Jennings Bryan (1860–1925) (b/w photo), American Photographer, (20th century) / Private Collection / Peter Newark American Pictures / Bridgeman Images: 163

William Jennings Bryan (1860–1925) speaking at a Democratic Convention, Chicago, 1896 (colour litho), American School, (19th century) / Private Collection / Peter Newark American Pictures / Bridgeman Images: 161